Best for Baby

A Selective Consumer's Guide
to Products and Services
From Infancy to Preschool

Shannon Gilligan and Susan Landsman

Longmeadow Press

We received generous help from a large number of people in assembling this project. Although we don't have space to thank them all, we would especially like to single out the following: Judy Woodruff, R.A. Montgomery, Mag Dusseau, Mary Ann Gilligan, Charles Fallick, Andrea Van Hoeven, Judy Sarrick, Earla Sue McNaull, Nancy Balaban, Jim Greenman, Nancy Lauter-Clatell, and Jane Shattuc. We would also like to thank the librarians of the Bailey Howe Library at the University of Vermont and the Fletcher Free Library in the city of Burlington.

—S.G. & S.L.

Cover Design: The Laughing Bear Associates
Book Design: The Laughing Bear Associates
Cover photo Copyright© Niki Mareschal/The Image Bank
Product photography, except when supplied by the
    manufacturer: Len Mastri
Day care photos courtesy of Shawn Connell and Jean Wambach

Table of Contents

How to use this Book

There are a bewildering number of new products and services that a prospective parent must learn about. *Best For Baby* is designed to make that job easier. We have looked at literally thousands of products and consulted dozens of experts in an attempt to identify the very best in products and services that are available for your new child today.

Each section contains an introduction that outlines safety features to watch for and pitfalls to avoid. For less tangible subjects like nannies, we have tried to provide enough information for parents to make educated judgments. In all sections we have listed resources for obtaining further information.

Product selection was based on the following criteria: innovative and practical design, quality of manufacture, and reasonable price. What we mean by reasonable price is a product worth the amount you pay for it. A number of fairly expensive products made it into this guide, but in our opinion, they are worth it. You will receive a fair return on your investment. We also tried to identify plain old good values in each category.

We have done our best to provide accurate pricing information and product descriptions. But of course both of these are subject to change. If you find a specific item that you cannot live without, the book finishes with a thorough shopping guide and in many cases numbers to call to locate a product in your area.

Best Cribs

Among the 3 or 4 million cradles now rocking in the land are some which the nation would preserve for ages as sacred things, if we could know which ones they are.

Samuel Clemens

Best Cribs

According to old illuminated manuscripts, cribs came into use sometime before the Norman conquest. These early versions were hollowed-out logs. Their naturally rounded shape was a bonus: it made them easy to rock. If there aren't any around today, it's probably because they were used for fire wood once their original purpose was outgrown.

Furniture makers kept that useful rocking feature. Medieval manuscripts depict cradles mounted on rockers inserted in the bottom of the crib structure, or even mounted to swing between two posts. These belonged to the upper classes. No one else could afford furniture.

By the sixteenth century, ideas of what would suffice for tots of noble birth had changed. "Cradles of Estate" were designed to reproduce in miniature the magnificence of royal beds. These were generally used for show, however. There was always a second crib—still opulent, of course—for practical use.

Designers and makers of furniture hung onto the rocking mechanism through the centuries. Sheraton, the famous English furniture designer of the late eighteenth century, featured a "Swinging Crib Bed" in his *Cabinet Dictionary*. It swung on its own by means of some clock gears. In a short while, this mechanism had been improved to the extent that it could rock a baby in a crib for up to an hour and a half. In Victorian England there was actually a category of nursery servant called "rockers." These people were employed full time to do nothing but swing an infant heir's cradle.

The predecessors of today's cribs came into being in the industrialized nineteenth century. Mass-produced cribs rolled off the assembly lines with some of the features of today's models. Collapsible cribs came into vogue back then, too. Infants during this period generally slept in a crib while tiny and graduated to a small child's bed as they grew larger.

Modern cribs have evolved to include elements of both older cribs and small beds. Cradles (which rock) have fallen into disuse.

The standard size of today's crib is 28 × 50 inches. The best ones are made of hardwoods and are covered with tough nontoxic enamels or sealants. Hardware should be sturdy, with no sharp edges. A plastic teething bar on crib rails is useful but not necessary.

The U.S. Consumer Products Safety Commission has two mandatory requirements: slats spaced 2 3/8 inches apart and a mattress that fits snugly on all four sides. Beyond that, they subject every crib to a strict engineering analysis and will force a recall of any product that might conceivably put your baby in danger. Despite these strict measures, it is a good idea to check with your crib salesperson that the item you're about to purchase is CPSC-approved.

A Crib Futon

A futon is a traditional Japanese mattress made of several layers of cotton batting encased in a sheath of cotton duck. Newer Americanized versions sometimes include a few layers of wool with the cotton for added firmness and support. For parents who have converted to this very comfortable and healthy sleep surface, and who would like their newborn to benefit from same, there are now crib-sized versions. The Burlington Futon Company in Burlington, Vermont will make one to order within twenty-four hours. They have three models to choose from: four layers of cotton batting for approximately $40, six layers of cotton batting for $50, and a cotton with wool core for approximately $65. They also welcome orders for accessories like bumpers and pillows. All cotton materials, both casing and batting, are treated with boric acid, a natural flame retardant. They guarantee their products unconditionally against manufacturing defects for the life of the product.

The Zenith

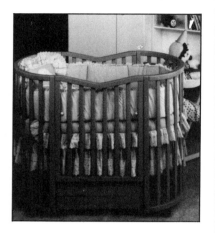

Zenith is a crib by Lewis of London, an American firm that has its cribs manufactured in Italy. The Italian workmanship shows: detail and finishing are exquisite. It has a single drop side. A double-knob adjustment lifts or lowers the rails. Some people prefer the "drop kick bar," which allows a parent to lift or lower the side with one hand (and one foot). In the **Zenith's** case, this lack is compensated for by three adjustable mattress levels. You probably won't have to let down the rails much anyway. Absence of such a bar underfoot also allows for two extra drawers underneath.

Like all Lewis of London cribs, this model is made of beechwood and weighs over 100 pounds. This is a fact you will appreciate as you go into stores and try shaking a few cribs. The weight really adds to its sturdiness and, in turn, according to owners, accounts for its long life.

It is also our opinion that the art deco design of **Zenith** makes it one of the sleekest-looking cribs around. It is available in white, natural, and gray. *Note*: Although the **Zenith** is standard size, its unusual oval shape means you'll probably have to buy their mattress as well. ***Suggested retail: $625.***

Rimini

The **Rimini** is imported from Italy by Tracers. It embodies wonderful Italian design in an unusual crib material: metal. The crib is thoroughly welded with a single drop side for additional stability. The **Rimini** is powder-coated. The enamel is applied as a powder and then baked on, almost like a clay pot being fired. This produces not only the toughest enamel finish, but the clearest colors as well. The crib has three adjustable mattress levels and a double knob release that is thoroughly childproof. Tracers guarantees their product against all defects of manufacture and assures that **Rimini** is CPSC-approved. Available in fire engine red, royal blue, and gleaming white. (Also available in light blue in certain markets.) ***Suggested retail: $270 to $300.***

Crib 'n Bed

Childcraft's **Crib 'n Bed** is a clever twist on the theme of the ordinary crib. It's designed with removable sides and headboard. As your baby grows, simply remove these and you have a child's daybed that's 68 inches long. The **Crib 'n Bed** features a hinged half rail on one side with a double-knob adjustment. While your baby is still an infant, you can probably leave this down. The piece is constructed of wood with plastic laminate covering. It comes with a boxspring that extends the length of the unit. Childcraft sells a mattress with extender for changing it into a regular bed. What we like best is all the drawer space. Available in a number of colors, as well as an oak finish. *Note:* The mattress used on **Crib 'n Bed** must be at least 5 inches thick. *Suggested retail: $660.*

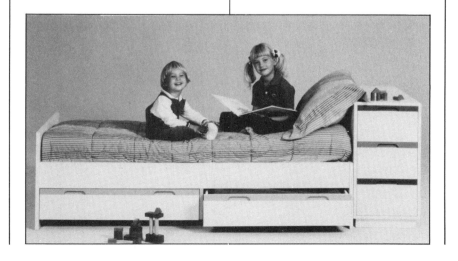

The Granada

The **Granada**, imported just this season by the Marshall company, is causing a stir in the industry. Unlike other cribs manufactured in Europe and brought to this country, it is European sized. European cribs are smaller. Because Americans, especially those inhabiting cities, are living in smaller and smaller spaces, we are convinced that the **Granada's** 22 3/8 × 46 1/8 inch measurements are the wave of the future. (Various sources attribute American crib size to the Depression when people wanted their child's first bed to last as long as possible, and thus made them larger.) Another advantage to its size beside more room in the nursery is that this crib can slide through a standard doorway. Changing your nursery into a real guest room is the work of a moment.

The **Granada** is superbly crafted to extremely high standards in Spain. It is available in white or the natural finish you see pictured. Marshall assures us that it passes all federal safety requirements. It possesses a single drop side with kick bar adjustment for lowering, and comes with its own 5-inch thick foam mattress. They have imported a full line of bedding and coordinated accessories that can be purchased separately. At last word, a number of U.S. bedding manufacturers were looking to get in on the act. *Approximate retail: $375.* Mattress and accessories are additional.

Best for Baby

The Country Crib

For the first time, Fisher-Price is producing a line of three cribs. We strongly suspect that it will live up to their reputation for producing top-quality children's products. The **Country Crib** featured here is made with solid hardwood construction. It fits the standard mattress, which can be adjusted to four heights, depending on your infant's age. Their innovation is a nifty one-hand button operation to lift or lower the rail. This crib will be available in two different finishes—dark maple or the honey maple pictured here. Each design has a coordinated dresser with hideaway changing top available separately. It looks more like a real dresser than any similar product we've seen.
Approximate retail: $350.

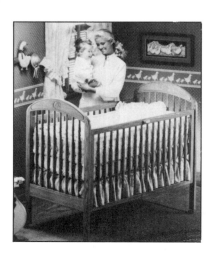

Palermo

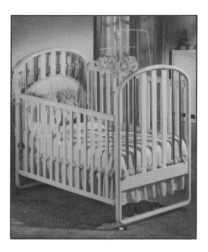

Palermo is our representative for the popular and well-made (in America) Simmons line. (They, along with Childcraft, are the two major U.S. manufacturers of cribs.) Like all Simmon's cribs, it is sturdily fashioned of northern hardwoods. The **Palermo** features double drop sides with a new patented push-button release that can be used with only one hand (leaving the other free for baby). It rides on heavy-duty, wide plastic casters that are kind to your floors. The crib reflects a European design influence with brass accent rails picked up in the wheel casings. **Palermo** comes in white or natural finish, and a variety of matching nursery furniture can accompany it.
Suggested retail: $340.

Travel Cot

In our opinion, the **Travel Cot** by Baby Björn of Sweden could almost double as a full-time crib. According to the U.S. distributors, in Sweden it is often used for just that. It is extremely stable in spite of weighing only 12 pounds and has been thoroughly tested for strength by the Swedish Furniture Testing Institute. It is also unusually easy to assemble. The 100% cotton covering can be removed and washed, vinyl "peeking window" and all. Because the mattress has a 100% cotton covering, it cannot be sold in this country. We suggest having one made by the Burlington Futon Company (see page 187). The **Travel Cot** is available in natural wood finish with a choice of lovely prints including a pinstripe or the one you see here in blues and greens. If you decide to use it as your main crib, it's a steal at this price.
Approximate retail: $180.

Sam's Crib

At the opposite end of the spectrum, and for parents who wish to spare no expense, there's **Sam's Crib** (or ones like it). This crib is made by hand of the finest cherry wood by master craftsman, Dan Moshein. While carefully adhering to CPSC standards, he used his own design sense. The outstanding result has a single drop side operating on a hinge principle and three mattress levels, in addition to the requisite 2 3/8 inch bar spacing. It also snugly fits the standard crib mattress.

The proud owners of **Sam's Crib** can be assured of two things: they will possess one of the prettiest cribs we've seen, and they will probably see their grandchildren in it. Details about how to order from Moshein directly (or about finding a furniture maker in your own area) can be found in the shopping guide. An added plus: he is happy to work with client input. *Retail: approximately $1500,* depending on wood and ornateness of design.

The Evelyn

The **Evelyn**, a collapsible crib, provides Lewis of London quality and design at a more affordable price. Made of beechwood like all Lewis cribs, it is slightly lighter to aid in portability. The unique collapse design operates on the diagonal. This allows for better stability when the crib is assembled. In fact, **Evelyn** as a collapsible is more stable than a good number of uncollapsible cribs on the market. It has three adjustable mattress levels and comes in gray or natural, as well as white. Sorry, no drop sides. *Suggested retail: $295.*

The Commuter

Many new parents balk at the idea and expense of a second portable crib for travel. That's until they have the baby. Then, according to many people we talk to, they run out to buy one on the first free Saturday.

They could do well to purchase **The Commuter** by Newborne. The crib is constructed from a powder-coated steel frame. It is covered in see-through nylon mesh with synthetic fabric trim. The mattress is a comfortable 2 inches of foam encased in vinyl. (You will probably want to add some natural fiber sheets.) To disassemble, you lift the mattress out, pull up on the concealed handle, and the **Commuter** folds up into a neat rectangle that then slips into its heavy nylon carrying bag. It weighs less than 16 pounds and can be used by babies up to two years of age. **Commuter** is available in light blue with a white frame or gray with a red frame. Mattresses are color coordinated. It even comes with its own mosquito net! *Suggested retail: $79.95.*

Lamby—A Last Thought

In the course of our research travels for this book, we ran across **Lamby** (pronounced "lammy"), and would like to give it an unqualified plug. Recent British research has shown that low birthweight babies in incubators gained weight faster than their peers when placed on a lambskin. Australian Mothercraft clinics have found that particularly restless babies settle down a lot more quickly on lamb fleece. Both these find-

ings are corroborated by American research that emphasizes the importance of tactile sensation in reducing tension. In short, few new products on the U.S. market can do as much to enhance your baby's quality of life as this one.

Lamby is the only *medical quality* lambskin currently available stateside. This means that it is tanned by a special, nontoxic process, standards for which are set by the Australian Wool Board. **Lamby's** U.S. distributor recommends placing a baby right on it with no sheet in between. In addition to the benefits listed above, it behaves like regular wool—warm in winter, cool in summer, and moisture absorbent—almost enough of a recommendation in itself. *Suggested retail: $50.*

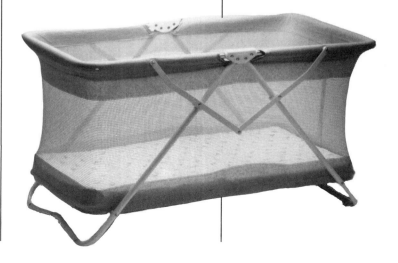

The Crib Alternative

A trend is gaining momentum among childcare experts and parents alike that eliminates cribs altogether. It is bringing your new baby into bed with you. Tine Thevenin argues in her book *The Family Bed* that separating children from their parents at bedtime has only happened in the past 200 years. She, along with a growing number of others, feel that the added security of such an arrangement produces happier kids. Parents who have started this practice refer to a hidden plus. When the child awakes in the night, one or both are right there to comfort it. Apparently, most children spontaneously give up the shared bed between the age of three and four when they're ready for some independence.

This whole idea may seem weird at first to many people, especially with the heritage of Freudian ideas we all seem to carry. Of course, the success of the shared bed depends on a full commitment from both partners. But don't dismiss it too quickly. We're all in favor of anything that produces happier and more confident children!

Choosing a Mattress

The two main types of mattress are foam and coil. Here are some buying tips for both and good examples.

SPRING MATTRESSES

Coil Construction

Heavy gauge wire is preferable (look for a low number like 13 or 14). Wire should also be double heat-tempered, which ensures that the steel will bend less over time. The coils should be locked in place (also called no-twist or offset) to decrease chances of denting in the middle. A border wire—about 9 gauge thickness—should tie the coils together. This tie helps distribute weight evenly and support the edges of the mattress, especially when your baby jumps or stands on the side. Many salespeople will try to promote a certain mattress according to the number of its coils. It's not the number but the quality of wire that counts.

Padding

Nonallergenic padding is preferable. Manufacturers use everything from horse hair to coconut fiber to cotton felt, so be sure to check. Good mattresses have two to three layers of padding: a synthetic fiber to wrap around springs and a polyurethane foam pad (often two layers of different densities) to wrap around that.

Outer Fabric

The best outer fabrics are reinforced vinyl laminates. Fabric is glued or melted into the vinyl during the manufacturing process. This process adds to durability and reduces stretching. It also renders a mattress tear-, stain-, and water-resistant.

FOAM MATTRESSES

The best foam mattresses are made from high-density foam. Some manufacturers buy seconds on foam and stuff it into mattresses. For this reason, we recommend going with a reputable name-brand company if this type of mattress is your choice.

Look for a mattress with edges sewn together with fabric tape instead of vinyl. It's better wearing. With either type of mattress a warranty is the thing to consider. Many top mattresses come with one that lasts fifteen years. If there's no warranty, that's a red flag.

Sealy Posturepedic Mattress

Gerry Baby Products is the sole distributor for Sealy Posturepedic mattresses. Their top-of-the-line is Sealy Ultra Premium Baby Posturepedic with Staph Bloc. This is an excellent coil mattress with a special covering treatment used by hospitals to resist bacteria. Fifteen year warranty. *Approximate retail: $79 to $89.* Their high-density foam mattress is the Sealy Support System 720, also with a fifteen-year warranty. *Approximate retail: $39.*

Firm 150 Heavy Duty Coil Design

Okla Homer Smith is a subsidiary of Gerber Products. They make the Firm 150 Heavy Duty Coil Design. *Approximate retail: $59.* They also make a 5-inch Poly-foam Deluxe mattress. *Approximate retail: $39.* Both have a three-year warranty.

Baby Beautyrest

Simmons manufactures the Baby Beautyrest. It features soft padding on the surface but a firm and resilient coil construction inside. *Approximate retail: $95.* Their best-selling mattress is the Super Maxi-pedic with 160 coils and a triple laminate cover. *Approximate retail: $75.* The Simmons Quo Foam is made from two blocks of foam rather than the traditional one. There's a 2-inch layer and a 3-inch layer, one side for infants and the other for toddlers. *Approximate retail: $60.* Simmons does not provide a warranty, per se, for their mattresses, but they do stand behind their products for defects.

Flotation Crib Mattress

Nature Baby in California manufacturers the Flotation Crib Mattress, or a water bed for infants. It has a wood support, then a slab of high-quality foam, a lap-seam mattress, a safety liner with built-in insulation, and finally a heavy-duty vinyl zippered "water envelope" cover. It holds 8 gallons of water and needs no heater because of the insulation. The idea is that the water motion and suspended sensation give a baby a more womblike feeling. They also claim it improves skin and head development because it doesn't resist body contours and allows the blood to circulate more freely. It comes with a fifteen-year warranty. *Retail: $109.*

Best
Playpens&Infant Seats

Best for Baby

Best Playpens & Infant Seats

The idea of a playpen must be repugnant to most parents. Today retailers almost universally refer to them as play *yards*. Of course the size has not changed; only the name has, and it creates a pleasant illusion in the mind of a buyer. In truth playpens are a useful and necessary child-rearing device. Babies need almost nonstop care and attention. And one person alone in a house will sometimes have to attend to a phone call or cook dinner. A playpen provides a safe place to put your child while your attention is required elsewhere. Experts assert that a playpen will have no undue effects on your child's worldview as long as you do not use it as a substitute for care. They advise making the playpen experience more interesting by putting in some favorite toys and changing the toys often.

Playpens come in two sizes. A standard one is usually 36 inches square. Deluxe models are 40 inches square (that's 11 square feet of play space). But your first choice will probably be material: wood or mesh. Wooden playpens should be constructed of hardwoods and have slats spaced 2 3/8 inches apart, just like cribs. Mesh playpens are lighter, collapsible, and therefore portable. Today they are by far more popular although some persons prefer wood because it enables their baby to see more. In either case, make sure that railings are at least 20 inches above the playpen floor. The best mesh pens have fully padded rails and legs, so your infant has nothing to hurt himself on in a fall. The Juvenile Products Manufacturers Association recommends playpens only for infants under 30 pounds and 34 inches tall. *Note*: If you opt for a mesh playpen, do not leave one side down for easier access as some folks have been wont to do. Infants have been caught in their space and suffocated or choked.

For very young infants, you may want to consider purchasing an infant seat. It functions similarly to a playpen in that it's a good way to keep your baby in a safe place while he's dozing or entertaining himself and you're doing something else. The advantage is that it doubles as a carrier: When you have to change rooms, just carry your baby with you. Many parents like to place the infant seat on the dining table with them to let their baby participate in mealtimes from the start.

Best for Baby

Thru-the-Door

This Kolcraft play yard has reduced width allowing it to be transported from room to room without being folded first, hence the name. It measures 24 × 38 inches and features safety lock hinges, a powder-coated frame, and hairpin curve feet for stability and delicate floors. The legs and rails are thickly padded and vinyl covered. The vinyl half-inch pad removes for wiping off. This playpen is a nice size for travel, weighing in at under 20 pounds. Available in navy. *Approximate retail: $60.*

40-Inch Activity Play Yard

This well-padded vinyl-and-mesh play yard has two built-in activities for your infant: a clock and a phone dial. Two sturdy pull-up rings will help your baby as he learns to balance and stand up. The press-button safety locks cannot be reached by curious fingers. The steel frame legs are contoured to protect rugs and floors. The play yard features an additional center leg support, close-weave polyester mesh, and a wide draft guard along the bottom. It also folds easily for storage or travel. Available in a sleek-looking "Grey Elegance" vinyl print from Century. *Approximate retail: $70 to $75.*

Travel Tender

This cross between a playpen and traveling crib is one of the most popular items in the Fisher-Price lineup. It is covered by a durable nylon fabric and comes with a separate foam mattress and measures 24 × 38 inches. **Travel Tender** has a solid floor and reinforced sides for baby's safety. It also has a center stabilizing foot. It all folds down into a neat package that can be fit in an accompanying carry sack. Fisher-Price also makes a similar full-sized playpen. Available in royal blue. *Approximate retail: $78.*

Folding 40 Deluxe Play Yard

This model was the only 100% fabric-covered play yard we found. It also has special telescoping legs that allow it to fold up to a compact 24-inch height. The cloth mattress pad can be removed and thrown in the wash. The play yard has no-pinch hinges, a center stabilising leg, and a hairpin curved steel frame to protect floor surfaces. Available in light blue gingham checks or periwinkle blue with coordinated pads from Gerry. *Approximate retail: $80.*

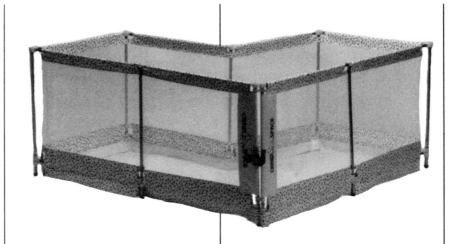

Century Crawlspace

This frame allows you to set up your own play area outdoors or in. Eight hinged sides can be set up in any configuration, creating 16 square feet of crawl space. The **Crawlspace** is sturdily made and the only one we found with a single continuous mesh side and no hinges exposed. It weighs less than half a regular playpen and folds down to a compact size. Parents tell us that it's perfect for the beach. *Note:* This item is good only up to 12 months, at which time your baby will be a proficient enough escape artist to get out of it. *Approximate retail: $30 to $35.*

Best for Baby

Wooden Playpen

For parents who would like a wooden playpen, we recommend this well-made model from the Rifton Community in Rifton, New York, an old Christian group that has its roots in the Reformation. It's built with a solid maple frame, 2 3/8 inch spaced slats, and folds for easy storage. The playpen's interior space is 35 × 37 inches in size. A 1-inch thick foam pad covered in vinyl-laminated nylon is sold separately. Available through the community's catalog, the two items together sell for $189.

Great Kid's Porta-Pad

Some playpen manufacturers have recently come out with extra fabric pads to cover the vinyl ones already in place, but this combination can be dangerous. Vinyl is slippery. Even if the fabric is anchored, it is bound to slip a bit. Just think of how frustrating this is to an infant learning to stand up! Instead we recommend **Porta-Pad** by the Great Kid Company. This 40 inch-square cushion is designed to fit all play yards. It is made from a thick, lightweight foam that is hypoallergenic and machine-washable. The special foam/fabric has a unique gripping surface that does not skid. It can be used without a playpen to define a play area. **Porta-Pad** comes in bright red, reversing to royal blue. We highly recommend it. *Approximate retail: $15 to $18.*

Snugli Bouncer Infant Carrier

This ingenious three-position infant seat has a special bouncing position that can be activated by your baby's movement, or your own touch. The upright position is convenient for feeding or looking, and the lowest position is perfect for carrying. The carrier features double handles that lock in both down and upright carrying positions. It comes with a washable padded cover in vinyl or fabric and special handholds in the bucket seat for easy portability. A restraining strap provides extra security, when necessary. White molded plastic body and two pastel patterns to choose from. *Note:* not available til April, 1988. *Approximate retail: $40.*

Tyke-Hike Baby Rocker

The natural rocking action of the **Baby Rocker** quickly calms an infant down. It features an extra-deep seat and an extra-wide stomach belt that snaps your baby securely into place. Small plastic restrainers can be rotated on the bottom rims to hold the seat steady. The Rocker's 50-50 polyester/cotton fabric can be removed for washing. A removable hood fits on top to protect your child from wind and sun, or drafts indoors. Best of all it folds up easily and weighs less than 5 pounds for toting on picnics, etc. Available in a wide range of primary colors or a grid pattern in primaries or electric pastels. *Note:* Recommended for newborns until they can pull themselves forward. *Approximate retail: $50.*

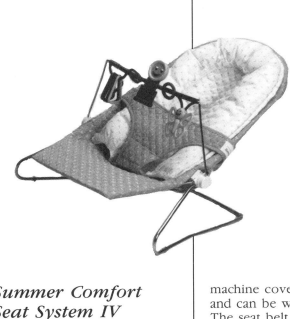

Summer Comfort Seat System IV

The Summer company worked with pediatricians and preschool educators to perfect the safest and most anatomically correct seat for young infants. It is designed to conform naturally to a baby's growing shape. Four layers of soft 100% cotton quilted fabric provide proper support to your baby's head, neck, and spine. The custom fabrics are sanforized to prevent shrinkage, hypoallergenic, and printed with special dyes that resist fading and bleeding. The machine cover removes easily and can be washed and dried. The seat belt adjusts in two directions to provide maximum safety. The flexible frame allows a gentle rocking motion as your baby gets heavier and acquires improved motor control. The system comes with a special support cushion for newborns. The height-adjusting educational toy bar provides early visual stimulation and later, increased motor play. All three pieces fit into a roomy travel pouch. Available in blue, green, or pink. The seat is also sold by itself. *Approximate retail:$60 to $70.*

Johnny Jump-Up Gym Seat

Babies just love these exerciser seats, which usually hang in doorways, providing a good view of all the action. We like this model made by Evenflo. It has foam-padded sides and seat and is made from extra-strong vinyl-laminated cloth, with nylon hanging straps. Jumping action helps strengthen babies' leg, back, and abdominal muscles, and increases coordination too. Good for infants from 4 months up until they weigh 24 pounds. It comes in white with teal blue accents. *Approximate retail: $19 to $22.*

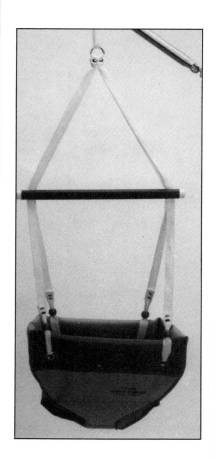

Best
Carriages & Strollers

Best for Baby

There followed a lighter carriage, and in this, as he spun along, he would tend to rise, straining at his straps; clutching at the edges; standing there less like the groggy passenger of a pleasure boat than like an entranced scientist in a spaceship; surveying the speckled skeins of a live, warm world.

Vladimir Nabakov, 1934

Best Carriages & Strollers

The first modern baby carriages were introduced on New York City streets in 1848. Pedestrians considered the unwieldy vehicles a nuisance. They weren't particularly soothing to infants either: early models had solid steel wheels and no shock absorbers in an age when streets and sidewalks were covered with cobblestones. Having no brakes, they were also a common cause of infant deaths.

Carriages probably would have disappeared entirely if Queen Victoria hadn't ordered them for her whole brood. Like all the other royal habits, this one was quickly copied. Soon the English had become the world's leading maker of baby carriages. By the turn of the century, they were introducing hundreds of new models annually. These later versions had elaborate bodies of wood or wicker and silk parasols to shield the sun. They rode high off the ground on 24-inch wheels, still mostly steel. Rubber wheels were available but cost extra.

Parents were still pushing around modified versions of these earlier prams (the word is a bastardization of the noun *perambulator*) as late as the 1960s. Ten years later, lightweight metals like aluminum and concepts like collapsibility had changed carriages and

strollers for good. Today few true carriages are manufactured. Instead designers have worked to include
the best features of strollers and carriages in a single
model that will last your baby's childhood. These
models have reclining seats, reversible handles, and
enclosable footrests that essentially transform a
stroller to a carriage for the few months that an infant
is small enough to require one. Consumer Product
Safety Commission standards are the same for both.
Wheels should be large enough for stability, and dual
wheels (a total of eight) are best. A stroller or carriage
should not tip, even with your child sitting as far back
as possible in the unit. Make sure that the brakes lock
tightly. Your carriage or stroller should have no sharp
or scissorlike mechanisms that can harm a child.
Wheel locks, which fix wheels into a straight-ahead
position, are a nice extra for times on uneven surfaces.

Best for Baby

Ringo

Bandaks/Emmaljunga makes the top of the line in baby carriages today. The carriages are manufactured in Sweden by Emmaljunga and imported to this country by Bandaks. If this carriage looks familiar, it's probably because it's the one used by oil jillionaires on "Dallas." We like their **Ringo** model, which can be operated like a pram then turned into a stroller as your baby grows. A separate bassinet is fitted onto the frame for the carriage mode. Remove the bassinet, make a few adjustments, and you have a stroller. (Incidentally, for times when your toddler wants to sleep, the stroller also reclines fully.) Height of the seat can be adjusted when you make the switch; this feature saves strain on your back.

The **Ringo** is covered in top-quality stretch gabardine and is luxuriously padded. A special shock-absorbing mechanism gives your baby a smooth ride. Weighing a hefty 40 pounds, this carriage has a nice solid feel. It's expensive compared to other carriages on the market, but the quality is well worth the price. The Ringo comes with an adjustible hood, the steel and rubber wheels have a lifetime guarantee, and it's available in nine different colors. *Note:* The **Ringo** is also available without the bassinet; in this mode it is called the **Ringo Sportcombi**. *Approximate retail: $350 to $440.*

The 911s

On The Town has named all its carriages after Porsches. We like the **911s**, which features an ultralight aluminum frame, telescopic reversible handle for carriage or stroller mode, and a neat mesh carrying bag that lets you collapse the stroller without having to move a cumbersome plastic or wire shelf first. This stroller also has a three-position reclining backrest that adjusts at the touch of a button. The seat, foot rest, and back rest are all molded plastic. They are covered by a removable and washable padded hammock. A three-position carriage-style hood will shield your baby from sun and other elements. Available in rose or blue. *Approximate retail: $125.*

Blue Candy Stripe

The **Blue Candy Stripe** from Kolcraft has a wide powder-coated frame that resists scratches. It has three recline positions, including a pram position. The handle flips over so your baby can face you. Underneath, it carries a vinyl-coated basket for groceries or diapers. Four sets of dual wheels and separate wheel suspension for each ensures control for the driver and comfort for the rider. The footrest is solid and the padding can be taken off and washed. Available in a blue frame with pink and white pinstripe bunting.
Approximate retail: $110.

Quattro Domani

Perego, the maker of this stroller, recently stole back a large share of the designer stroller market from Aprica by providing a better product at a better price. Indeed they have been in the business longer. Perego had dominated the northeastern luxury market for almost twenty years. Today they are distributed nationally from the midwest. The line is designed in Italy and uses Italian fabrics but is manufactured here in the United States.

The **Quattro Domani** offers a lightweight powder-coated chassis on front and *rear* swivel wheels. (This makes it easier to steer when you are using the pram mode.) The padded restraining bar comes off for easy access. Likewise the safety belt has a push-button release. The reversible handle has an automatic locking feature. The fabrics are weather-resistant, and the stroller comes with a full canopy hood and under-basket. The **Quattro Domani** has wonderful shock absorption and folds easily. Available in gray, green, or blue.
Approximate retail: $130 to $140.

Best for Baby

Silver Shadow Esprit

Alkot was the first manufacturer to introduce quilted upholstery to a collapsible stroller. Today they are still noted for their luxurious and comfortable look. The collapsible **Esprit** comes with a reversible and adjustable handle. The padded boot that acts as a bunting when you are using the pram option comes off and changes into a diaper bag to hang on the rear of the seat. The stroller comes with front dual swivel wheels that lock, a padded front body rail, and wire underbasket. All pad-

ding removes for washing. Available in silver with or periwinkle blue accents. A mint-green version comes with a rain slicker in lieu of the diaper bag bunting.
Approximate retail: $119.

The Maclaren Dreamer

The dreamy aspect to this stroller is its weight: a mere 13 pounds. It also features an innovative design by a company famous for its high quality. Rather than flipping the handle to make it into a pram, you flip the seat. It locks into five different positions for infant comfort. In its stroller configuration, you have seven positions to choose from.

Meanwhile the front wheels remain the same, providing the same steering ability. The vinyl-laminate fabric seat is especially deep and comfortable. Your baby is strapped into place with a five-point nylon harness. The shopping tray underneath is oversized and solid plastic. The powder-coated frame is heavy-duty aluminum. Amazingly, this gear all folds down to a mere 8 inches in width. Available in blue gray or mint gray with appropriate accents.
Approximate retail: $200.

Jane/Janette

The **Jane** stroller is imported from Spain by the same outfit that brings in the Dreamer. It provides four reclining positions. The backrest operates simultaneously with the footrest, giving your baby proper orthopedic position and comfort. The padding is removable and washable. All four sets of dual wheels lock. The matching canopy has a see-through window to allow a view of your child. An optional carry cot called the **Janette** changes this model into a true pram. **Jane** weighs only 16½ pounds and folds down to a smidgeon of its full size. Available in light blue or gray. *Approximate retail: $200. Janette Carrycot: $80.*

Double Fold 'n Go II

If you already have a child with another on the way, you might consider the **Double Fold 'n Go**. Each seat features a separate recline. Like most of today's collapsibles, the handle flips for carriage capability. The 6-inch wheels are slightly larger than most for more stability. All four wheels lock and contain an individual suspension mechanism for comfort and smoothness. Both the canopy and footrest adjust. Available in navy with light blue accents. *Approximate retail: $130.*

A Note on Aprica

Five years ago, Aprica arrived from Japan and took the country by storm. Almost overnight they became the status stroller of choice. Today they have been weakened by a strong yen to the point they can no longer compete. Some Aprica models cost three times more than comparable models by other manufacturers. They still deliver a top-quality product, but so do many companies. Aprica is looking to shift manufacture to Taiwan or even Mexico. Until they make a move and bring their prices down, we recommend that you look elsewhere.

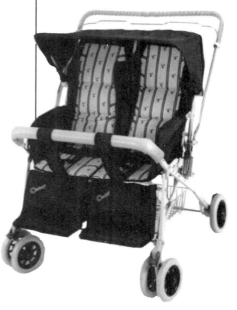

Famous Carriage Scenes From Film and Literature

1. *The Importance of Being Earnest*

In this Oscar Wilde play, Miss Prism (the nurse) leaves the baby Jack Worthing in a railway station locker by mistake. She then places her manuscript in the perambulator and prepares to set off.

2. *Battleship Potemkin*

One of the most famous carriage scenes in art occurs in this 1925 film by Sergei Eisenstein. A crowd of Odessa townspeople gather to protest the Czar's repressive rule, and the murder of a sailor in particular. As the Czar's army advances on the crowd and attempts to quell "the spirit of the people," they disperse, but not before a woman with a baby carriage is shot. Her falling body forces the carriage down the steps in one of the most extended and suspenseful scenes in early movie history.

3. *The Untouchables*

Brain de Palma pays homage to the scene described above in this 1987 film. This time the suspense occurs in Chicago's Union Station during a shoot-out between Eliot Ness and one of Al Capone's thugs. An innocent woman dragging a carriage up the steps is caught in the crossfire and loses hold of her precious cargo. Ness manages to capture the carriage and the criminal just in time.

4. *Gone With the Wind*

In a key transition scene, Rhett and Scarlet promenade up the street pushing their new baby Bonnie in an elaborate carriage made to look like it's horse-drawn. It is their attempt to reintroduce themselves to and become accepted once again by the southern aristocracy that has shunned them both, but particularly Rhett for his gambling past.

5. *Penny Serenade*

In George Steven's 1941 movie, Irene Dunne and Cary Grant adopt a child. Fate takes a cruel turn, and they are forced to return the child they have come to love. In one of the all-time great tearjerking scenes, Cary Grant goes about picking up the child's favorite toys, a toy carriage prominent among them, in order to take him back to the orphanage.

6. *Arthur*

In a hilarious scene from this 1981 film, Dudley Moore visits Liza Minnelli's apartment complex totally drunk. He runs into an empty baby carriage, looks bleary-eyed into it, and coos at a nonexistent baby. He next knocks on the wrong door, which prompts a quarrel among the couple that lives there. He goes back to the carriage and pulls a coverlet over the "baby" saying, "You shouldn't have to hear this."

Best Car Seats

Best for Baby

There are two classes of travel—first class, and with children.

Robert Benchley

Best Car Seats

ar seats were not originally designed for safety. They were made for the convenience of the parent. To ensure a parent's peace of mind, it was a common practice during the fifties and sixties to strap a child in a flimsy plastic shell hooked over the seat with a restraining mechanism that had the strength of a shoelace. This minimal restraint prevented a child from roaming freely and possibly playing with door handles or Mommy's hair. As recently as 1978, not a single state had a mandatory car seat law, despite the fact that car accidents were one of the leading causes of infant deaths.

Today this attitude has changed. All fifty states and the District of Columbia have some sort of car seat law. As of January 1, 1981, all car seats are subjected to stiff federal regulations for safety. Unfortunately, this law has not yet made car seats universal. According to studies by the Insurance Institute for Highway Safety, compliance with the new laws is still dismally low.

We cannot urge the use of a car seat strongly enough. A small infant unrestrained (and especially sitting on an adult's lap in the front seat) is at incredible risk. People who blithely point to their spotless driving record should note that 25% of all infant car injuries are caused by sudden stops or swerves. Moreover, research indicates that children introduced to a car seat from infancy are quieter and tend to fight and distract the driver less than those who have not.

There are several types of car seats to choose from. Infant car seats are designed to face backward. They tend to be lighter and portable, which is handy when you want to carry a slumbering infant into the house. They frequently have extra padding.

A convertible car seat is the most common and practical type. This car seat can be installed facing the rear for infants, and turned around once your child is older and weighs more than 20 pounds. These car seats are generally less portable.

When your child outgrows his car seat, booster-type seats for ages 4 to 7 are available. After that, your child is considered safe with a regular seatbelt.

A car seat must be installed properly to work. All seats are attached to the car by safety belts but be sure to follow manufacturer's instructions when threading the belts through. If you're unsure that your seat is correctly installed, take it back and check installation with the salesperson who sold it to you. Beyond that, make sure your car seat is wide enough for your child to grow and to accomodate bulky winter gear. Check to make sure that the harness buckles work easily and that the harness can be adjusted to fit snugly. It's good, but not necessary, to have a fabric covering instead of vinyl, which is hot in summer and cold in winter.

Carry it often in the arms, and dance it, to keep it from rickets and other diseases.

Jane Sharp

Best for Baby

Ultra Ride

We can imagine this car seat zooming past us in a Porsche. Its sleek design makes it appropriate for fancier cars, but it's also a good car seat. Kolcraft's **Ultra Ride** has no metal parts that will damage upholstery. It is a toddler seat that faces forward with two reclining positions. The five point harness system is recognized as safest in a crash. The fabric can't be removed, but it is treated to resist stains. Made in the U.S.A. Available in black with gray tweed and red harness. *Approximate retail: $65 to $80.*

Special Touring Edition 2000

The S.T.E. **2000** by Century has a particularly deep seat with high sides to give it lateral impact protection. As a convertible, it is good for both infants and toddlers up to 40 pounds. The soft terrycloth pad can be removed and washed. A built-in carry handle makes it easy to carry. The strap adjustments are conveniently located in front and noticeably easy to use compared to other car seats. The single button release also works well. The S.T.E. 2000 has three reclining positions and comes in a gray-blue tweed, blue hopsack, or neutral gray terry. *Approximate retail: $60 to $70.*

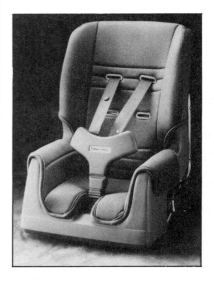

Fisher-Price Carseat

This is the best-selling car seat in the industry. It is a convertible: both rear and forward facing. There are three reclining positions for toddlers. Fisher-Price redesigned the restraining shield this year so it is scooped out and more comfortable. This shield has an inner spring that enables it to hug your child's chest. The straps adjust automatically to whatever clothing your baby has on and can be rethreaded when your child grows a size. The pad is made from actual car seat upholstery fabric and comes off to be laundered. It has a single-button release and weighs 15 pounds. A well-designed product that earns its stars. Available in blue. *Approximate retail: $78.*

GT 2000

This is an unusually well-padded car seat and sleek looking besides. It converts from birth to 40 pounds. A unique recline system allows for ten different positions. The plastic base is kind to upholstery. The fabric cover comes off; it has a side pocket for kid stuff. The **GT 2000** by Strolee has a super-safe five point harness restraint and is available in an understated blue or gray stripe. *Approximate retail: $90.*

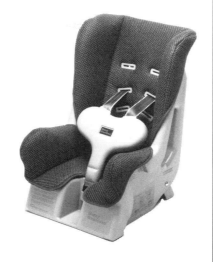

Guardian 653

The **Guardian** by Gerry is another excellent full-featured convertible car seat. Your child moves easily in and out, the straps adjust snugly, and it can be placed in the car properly with a minimum of fuss. It's another deep seat with good side protection and a removable fabric pad that exceeds many standards set by the FMVSS and is FAA approved. Available in gray with navy tweed or beige with brown tweed. *Approximate retail: $80.*

Seven Year Carseat

The scientifically designed **Seven Year Carseat** by Evenflo is the ultimate in practicality. It can be installed facing the rear, turned around for toddlers, and partially dismantled to provide a booster seat for older children. It is constructed from molded high-impact plastic and steel tubing. The shield and straps easily adjust, and the padding comes out to be washed (for a car seat that lasts this long, this feature is essential). Available in a lovely dotted blue velour. *Approximate retail: $85 to $100.*

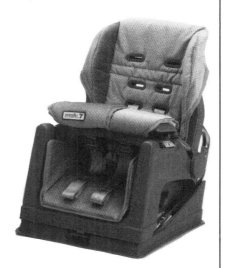

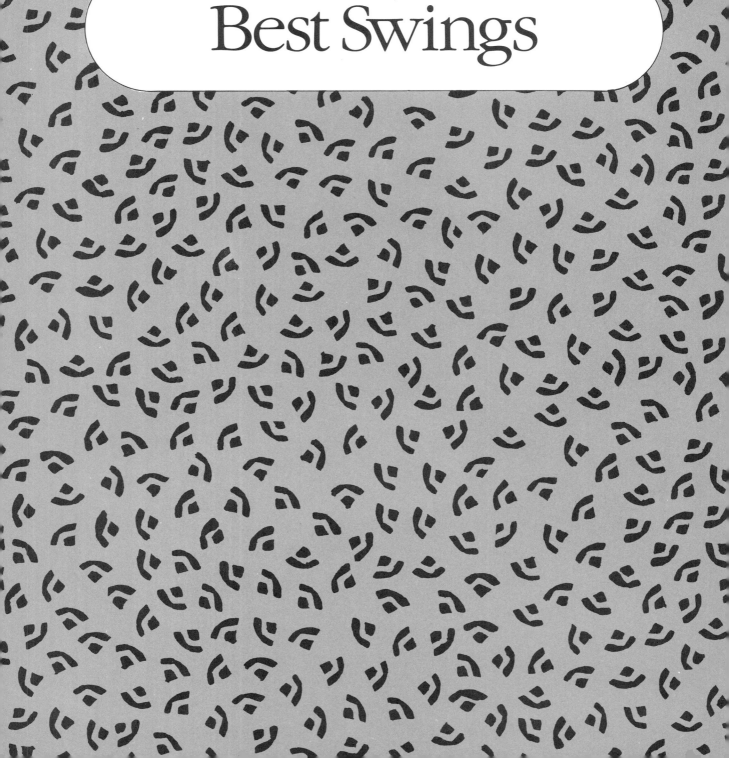

Best Swings

Best Swings

Even though a swing can be used for just the first six months, it is an extra that many feel is worth the price. The motion seems to have a magic effect on cranky infants and makes happy babies even happier. Doctors and other childcare experts suspect that the back and forth motion most closely approximates the womb experience in the outside world. After sucking, it appears to be an infant's favorite activity.

The swing can function as an excellent alternative to a playpen or bassinet for a very young child—it permits a parent to carry on with other household activities while they know their infant is content and in a safe place.

There are a number of swings to choose from. They operate by a wind-up mechanism or battery-powered motor housed in the top of the unit. When purchasing a swing, be sure to check noise levels of the swing in operation and, *more important*, the noise created to start it up. The motion of a swing often puts infants to sleep, and the principle is defeated if you have to wake the child every time the swing is reactivated. Beyond these checks, make sure that the unit is sturdily built and either folds or comes apart easily for times you'd like to store it. All good swing seats come with a restraining belt. Make sure your infant wears it at all times.

*When a voice behind me whispered low,
"That fellow's got to swing."*

Oscar Wilde

*Would you like to swing on a star,
Carry moonbeams home in a jar?*

Anon.

Best for Baby

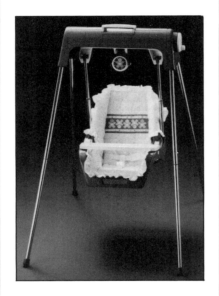

Fisher-Price Port-A-Swing

This is a wind-up swing that the company guarantees for two kids or five years, whichever comes first. It has a detachable infant seat that can double as a rear-facing car seat. The seat has two positions on the swing and three elsewhere. For parents concerned with safety, the seat also has a restraining belt and front detachable tray. The fabric pad removes for laundering. What we like best about the Fisher-Price is its combination of sturdy construction and easy portability. The swing can be folded flat to stow in a closet, or the legs can be dismantled and then snapped into the top

housing for trips away from home. We also found that the wind-up mechanism had a comforting ticking sound. It comes in royal blue and chrome. *Approximate retail: $70 to $80.*

Sing 'n Swing

By Strolee, this is a well-made swing for an excellent price. It contains a battery-powered motor that is nearly silent, and a music box that will play eight different tunes and may be adjusted separately or turned off altogether. The seat is vinyl or fabric and comes in eight different patterns that coordinate with

the powder-coated teal-blue legs. Another nice feature is swing arms made from nylon webbing instead of metal. *Note:* Two D batteries must be purchased separately. *Approximate retail: $65.*

Evenflo Swing/ Carseat/Carrier

All the features on this swing make it an excellent value, but what makes it special is a revolutionary new swing arc, unlike any other on the market. Other swings go back and forth, following the arc of a perfect circle. Instead this swing follows the pattern of an oval, giving a movement that more closely resembles

being rocked in human arms. Combined with all the options and an unusually strong and sturdy base, this is arguably the best swing on the market. The heavily padded seat reclines to four positions and the restraining belt is top quality; it covers shoulders as well as lower body and has a seatbeltlike buckle. The seat is lightweight and removes easily to be used as a rear-facing car seat or infant seat in another part of the house. Available in gray with red accents. *Approximate retail: $90 to $105.*

Graco Easy Entry Swyngomatic with Music

This product made its debut a little over a year ago and quickly became star of the season. The **Swyngomatic** runs up to 150 hours on two D batteries. The motor has a variable speed adjustment and a music synthesizer that can be turned on and off. Your baby is held in place by a nylon web restraining belt and and a tray that lifts off with two fingers. The seat reclines to two positions, and the angled arms enable the seat to remain steady while you're loading the cargo. Graco, which manufactures a line of high quality,

reasonably priced baby goods, used mothers and infants to design this product, and it shows. This year's model employs a quick disconnect feature that lets you disassemble the swing in under one minute. It comes in white with navy padding, ice blue with peach, or eggshell with mauve. A wind-up model is also available. Depending on wind-up or battery, fabric or vinyl, *approximate retail: $40 to $60.*

Sound Starter with Kanga Rocka Roo

This swing from Century has a unique sound-activator mechanism that responds to your infant's cry with three

minutes of swinging and then automatically shuts off. The swing can be activated separately, of course, with the press of a button (you do not have to start the swing in motion by hand, which is nice for sleeping infants). It operates for up to 150 hours on five D batteries. The **Kanga Rocka Roo** is actually an infant seat that easily lifts out and can be transported by a sturdy carrying handle. It has a front tray that can be taken off for access. The padding comes off too for washing. Available in a white frame with primary accents. *Note*: This swing is recommended only up to 17 pounds as opposed to the usual 22. *Approximate retail: $85.*

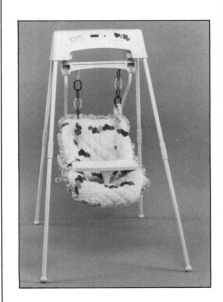

Best Carriers

Best Carriers

Aside from the papoose board used by native Americans, baby carriers did not exist on these shores until the late 1960s. A young couple returned from a stint in the Peace Corps in West Africa where they had noticed the local women carrying serene babies to market inside shawls tied to their backs. About to have their own child, Ann and Mike Moore asked Ann's mother, a seamstress by profession, to design and make a carrier like the one they remembered seeing. Other parents admired the Moores' carrier and asked for it. Ann's mother was soon making nothing else. By 1972, they had a full-fledged business on their hands, so Mike quit his job to form Snugli, Inc. Today the name Snugli has virtually become the generic term for a soft infant carrier.

There are two types of carrying pouches: one for the front and one for the back. The former is good for newborns and infants up to about 12 or 15 pounds. For babies over this weight, it is easier and better for your spine to carry your baby on your back. Back carriers often come with light metal frames for more structure and support. But they can only be used for older infants. Many soft carriers can be used on your back as well as front, so be sure to ask. When purchasing an infant carrier, also look for the following. Seams should be double-stitched, especially around fasteners and shoulder straps. Check to see whether you have to put the baby in the carrier first, or whether you can put it on before your baby goes in. If you are shopping for a newborn, make sure the carrier has head, neck, and back support. Good additional features are a snap-on bib to keep the carrier clean and inside zippers for nursing. *Note:* Never use your carrier in the car or in any activity that requires balance, like riding a bicycle.

Held Babies Are Happier Than Isolated Ones:

Some indigenous form of the Snugli exists throughout Asia, Africa, and South America. Recently researchers returned from studying the !Kung tribe in southwest Africa, a people who are known for holding their young offspring almost constantly. They found that !Kung babies cried 43% less than their American counterparts!

Snugli Original

This is the original **Snugli** model, and it continues to set the standard for the industry. Cross-strap construction balances your baby's weight. Quick-release plastic buckles make it easier to slip on and off than earlier versions. This **Snugli** is based on a double-pouch design, with your baby sitting in an inner adjustable seat that fits within the larger covering pouch. This model is designed for infants from newborns to 24 months and has a limited three-year warranty (which works out to be comfortably beyond the time your baby will use the carrier). There are leg and arm holes in the outer pouch for growing toddlers. This **Snugli** can also be worn on your back as your child gets heavier. The carrier comes with breastfeeding cut-outs and is fully machine-washable. Available in royal blue corduroy, blue pinstripe seersucker, and gray with color-coordinated linings. *Approximate retail:$55 to $60.*

The Safe Baby Carrier

This less-enclosed baby carrier by Baby Björn is perfect for summertime infants. The upper carrying strap actually goes under a baby's arms to provide plenty of back and head support. It also prevents a baby from falling out. There are wide padded shoulder straps for parents and a double-action safety buckle that can't be undone accidentally. The carrier comes with a snap-on drool bib and is machine-washable. Available in two-toned blue, or a light pink, or blue teddy bear pattern. *Approximate retail: $56.*

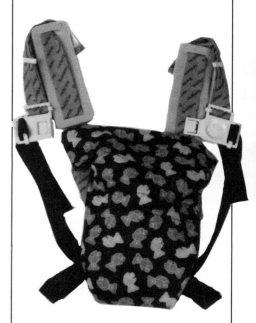

Snugli Soft Infant Carrier

Here is another model from **Snugli** designed especially for infants. It has three-ribbon adjustment for comfort and redesigned straps for better weight distribution. The straps are fully padded and have quick-release buckles. The arm and leg openings can be used by infants up to 9 months. Available in light blue with yellow ribbons and contrasting lining or gray stripe. *Approximate retail: $18.*

Sara's Ride

Sara's Ride is unique in that your baby rides at your side along your hip. This allows your upper torso to carry no more that 25% of the baby's weight. Another plus is a clear view of everything on the ground in front of you. The carrier provides easy access for nursing mothers too. The manufacturer suggests occasionally switching hips. The carrier has heavy-duty steel buckles, except near your infant's face where the buckle is plastic, and is made from strong cotton canvas with polypropylene webbing straps. **Sara's Ride** can also be used on your front or back and is suitable for infants from 4 months to 4 years. Available in blue. *Approximate retail: $24.95*

Best for Baby

Woven Palm Leaf Carrier

This woven carrier for small infants is made by Liepold of West Germany, one of the oldest and highest-quality wicker and palm manufacturers in the world. The 13 × 30-inch carrier has a reinforced top and bottom and reinforced handles. It has an adjustable hood held up by carriage-quality hardware. This is the largest and deepest palm basket we found. It is available in a variety of fabrics including a lovely eyelet pattern. It may not be as practical as some carriers, but it's lovely for occasions and as a tiny infant day cot. For siblings we recommend the 10 × 22-inch doll model. *Approximate retail: $69 to $129 depending on fabric. Doll carrier: $22.*

Colt

This is a frame carrier, designed for older and heavier children. Manufactured by Tough Traveler, a small, high-quality backpack outfit that has poured thousands of hours of climbing experience into the design of a carrier that can be used every day. The shoulders are padded with foam that rebounds under a 60-pound load. A sturdy waist belt, also padded, holds the carrier in place. The **Colt** has a quick-release buckle and adjusts to fit heights 5′ 2″ to 6′ 1″. It comes with a comfortable chair-shaped seat, infant restraining harness, a roomy carrying pocket, and fold-out support stand. *Note:* Tough Traveler makes an even sturdier model for hard-core mountaineers. Available in royal blue nylon with a red accent. *Approximate retail: $58.*

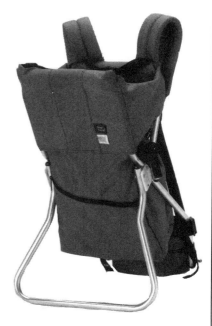

Carta-Kid

Carta-Kid, a carrier designed for shopping carts, was the ingenious invention of The Great Kid Company. Their motto is "Problem solving products for parents and kids," and they live up to it. **Carta-Kid** is made from a heavy foam-type fabric and secures a small infant comfortably and safely lengthwise in the shopping cart seat. As your child grows, the carrier transforms into a sitting version. The **Carta-Kid** is color-coded for its two modes: red for infant seat, blue for toddler. Recommended by pediatricians and every parent who's ever tried to shop another way. *Approximate retail: $16.95 to $19.95.*

Cozy Toes Carry Cot

By Baby Björn, this device is really a cross between a carrier for new infants and a portable crib. If it fits inside your stroller, it can double as a bassinet that your infant may sleep in. When your baby outgrows **Cozy Toes**, you may slip the sturdy support board out and use it as a stroller bunting. It comes with rugged carrying straps and double zippers. Available in light or navy blue, or bordeaux red. *Approximate retail: $140.*

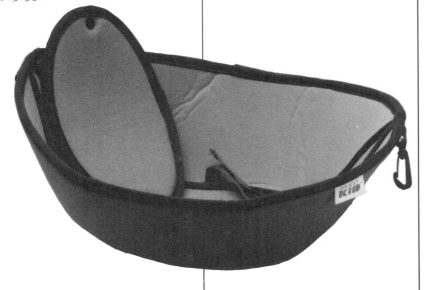

Gerry Portable Kiddie Seat

This is a simple frame carrier. It has adjustable foam padded shoulders with extra-wide straps. The nylon web hip support helps distribute weight evenly on shoulders and lower torso. The cotton blend contoured seat can be taken off and washed. The aluminium frame also snaps apart in seconds to be folded flat for travel. *Approximate retail: $32.*

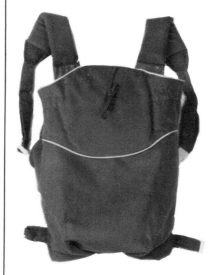

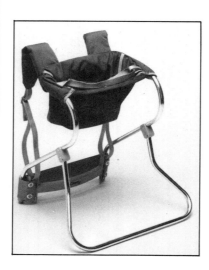

Cuddlepack

The **Cuddlepack** by Gerry is a full-featured well-made carrier at an excellent price. It comes with the standard padded shoulders and quick-release buckles. It also contains a spit-up bib, nursing zippers, and adjustable inner seat with infant back support. The opening is along the side to provide easier baby access both in and out. The **Cuddlepack** can be switched into a back carrier as soon as your infant is old enough. *Approximate retail: $40.*

Best Diapers

Best for Baby

Best Diapers

Before 1900, in warmer climates, babies' bottoms were left uncovered. Where there was a chill in the air, babes were swaddled in bands of cotton cloth. These swaddling clothes were often covered by knitted wool soakers. Eskimo and Indian cultures used absorbent plant materials, like peat moss, to prevent leakage onto clothes and parents.

In the 1950s, plastic pants and their sidekick, diaper rash, became standards in baby's wardrobe. Although throw-away diapers made their debut in 1933, it wasn't until the mid-sixties that they reached stardom. Disposables appeared in diaper bags and changing tables across the country. The marketing strategy was dryness with lots of talk about a "one-way barrier that keeps dryness in and lets moisture out." By 1985, Americans were using 16 billion disposables per year.

Disposable is certainly the key word. Critics of our "convenience culture" say that these disposables pose a serious environmental threat. Not only are we throwing away 90 million pounds of untreated fecal matter a year, but we're also making 600,000 additional tons of waste a year when we toss the diapers! And they'll be around a while: a disposable thrown on a trash pile today won't completely dissolve until sometime in the twenty-third century.

What's the key to such longevity? Typical ingredients are cellulose (wood) fiber, a synthetic top sheet, a hydrophobic surface, polyethylene film barrier (ethylene compounds are also used as fuel, anesthetics, or as ripeners of fruit), chemical binders, and artificial scent. There's more bad news: recent studies reveal the paper used in these diapers may contain dioxins, one of the most toxic organic chemicals known. Air and waste residue contaminated by dioxins have caused serious illness; even in small amounts, they have been linked to cancer in animals.

All these ingredients, benign and otherwise, produce a diaper that acts like a sponge. If you squeeze a wet one, the urine squishes out. The infamous one-way barrier works only if your baby never sits, lies down, or gets a loving squeeze. Bewildered parents with puddles on their pantlegs at first think either their baby's legs are too skinny to prevent leaks or their bladders are particularly prolific.

But in the eighties, diaper manufacturers have come clean and are the first to draw this leakage problem to our attention because now they have a solution—superabsorbants. The new diapers are expected to catch 75% of the 3.5 billion dollar disposable-diaper market. They're half as thick as regulars and so take up less space in baby carriers, dresser drawers, and grocery shelves. They hold at least twice the moisture; in fact, they lock it in. About a half tablespoon of sodium polyacrylate crystals, which can absorb fifty times their own weight, go into each diaper. These crystals, a synthetic compound also used in laxatives, pill coating, and sanitary napkins, turn liquid into gel, drawing moisture away from the baby's skin.

They're muscle builders too. This 2-ounce diaper can hold at least 10 ounces of urine and still feel dry. Unsuspecting parents watch adoringly as their 20-pound tots crawl around lugging another 5% of their body weight in the form of this mysterious gel.

Consumer groups have raised questions about the magical properties of these crystals. Will the gel that forms adhere to the baby's skin when the diaper is off? Will the crystals leech natural moisture away from

Best for Baby

Luvs by Procter & Gamble have been considered by some to be the Cadillac of diapers. They have extra padding up front, a streamlined middle to reduce bulk between the legs, an elasticized waistband, and five leg gathers to prevent leakage. The special waist panels, imprinted with Sesame Street characters, allow you to refasten tapes without tearing the plastic cover. *Price: $9.99 for 48 ultrathin mediums.*

Huggies by Kleenex also have an elasticized waist for those gravity-defiant piddles and tape that will refasten anywhere on the diaper. *Price: $9.89 for 48 mediums.*

Pampers by Procter & Gamble have long been the best sellers. These have a blue ribbon waist shield to keep moisture from seeping onto clothes. They also have an hourglass shape but seem slightly bulkier than Luvs. *Price $9.99 for 48 mediums.*

Warning: There have been documented cases of babies choking to death on the stuffing they pull out of their diapers. Parents are now advised to put pants on babies in disposables to prevent them from getting into the stuff.

skin, increasing the risk of infection or inflammation by removing body fluids? Some hospitals believe they over absorb and have refused to use them. The New York State Attorney General's Office is conducting an active investigation and the Food and Drug Administration has given a docket number to a petition filed by the Empire State Consumer Association claiming that the polyacrylate crystals can absorb interstitial fluid (the fluid between cells), causing the cells to dry up and the skin to shrivel.

But, and this is a big but, during two and a half years of nearly 7000 diapers, it's hard to resist disposables. Smelly, squirming babies are dry and adorable in seconds; and although they all have garbage pails, we've never seen a restaurant or hotel equipped with a diaper bucket. One mother of two in diapers, having had her fill, tossed a dozen cloth diapers out a Central Park West third story window. It just goes to prove that most of us need to use throw-aways, at least from time to time.

There are several brands and various features to choose from. The standard model has a smooth liner that draws wetness away, an absorbent inner padding, a thin plastic cover, and refastenable tapes. Different brands boast shapes that cut down on the bulk between baby's legs, extra elastic leg gathers, and printed plastic covers. The French, with their flair for romance, have a diaper that seranades the little one whenever she or he wets. We don't believe it's available on these shores. In the meantime, here's a rundown on some of our more conventional American models.

Note: If you plan to entrust your years in the diaper domain to one of these manufacturers, you'll dispose of about $1700 of your disposable income.

The Cloth Alternative

Though once the choice of the old-fashioned, salt-of-the-earth types, cloth diapers have become the new alternative. Pin pricks and rubber pants are passe: the all-in-one cotton and nylon variety, or terry diapers with velcro-fastening wool covers are state of the art. The argument for cloth is it's pure, porous, and baby soft. Cotton absorbs moisture but allows air to circulate to the skin. It lets out ammonia that's formed in the bacterial breakdown of urine. In fact, cotton binds in surrounding toxins, the reason why it has long been used for bandaging open wounds. These properties are supposed to save poor innocent babies from that chafing, itching monster: diaper rash.

Of course, that's a topic of controversy. Proponents of disposables claim that they carry no residues of bacteria or washing chemicals as cloth can, thus reducing the risk of irritation. The new superabsorbents actually bind the urine; manufacturers say this will prevent diaper rash.

Cotton lovers, on the other hand, say the disposable industry has convinced us that genital-area rash (commonly, albeit inaccurately, known as diaper rash) is an inevitable by-product of babyhood. Not so. A 1979 study in the Journal of Pediatrics showed that infants in disposables are five times more likely to have serious skin irritation. Since these diapers aren't breathable, they raise the baby's body temperature significantly, as much as 4 to 6 degrees. This alone is aggravating; combine it with wetness and the bacterial breakdown of urine—voilà—diaper rash. Babies in disposables may be changed less often because they appear to be dry, thus increasing the odds for discomfort. Lest we unfairly accuse the diaper (cloth or plastic), genital-area rash can be caused by other factors entirely, like food allergies, baby powders, and medicated baby wipes.

A soggy cloth diaper may seem more uncomfortable than a deceivingly dry disposable, but you're not in an absorbency marathon. The object is to keep the urine off you, the couch, and the rug. Then you change the diaper to keep the baby dry. Some of the latest in cloth diapers makes this procedure reliable, quick, and soft to the baby.

Washing Cloth Diapers

First rinse out wet or soiled diapers in the toilet or sink. Soak them in the diaper pail with baking soda and simple borax to disinfect. Lining the pail with a plastic bag keeps odors to a minimum and prevents mildew in hard-to-clean crevices of the pail. (We don't recommend the round diaper pail deodorizers that fit on the inside of the lid. These may contain a poisonous, cancer-causing agent.) Soak the diapers overnight in the washing machine with a baby detergent like Dreft and a mild commercial soaking solution like borax and run them through the hottest wash cycle.

Put the diapers through one or two additional hot-water rinse cycles. Use a quarter cup of baking soda or vinegar for softness and a fresh smell. Vinegar also gets rid of soap residues and prevents diaper rash. Avoid fabric softeners or antistatic paper sheets in the dryer; they contain irritating chemicals. If genital-area rash does develop, consider the following problems. Your detergent may be too strong or there's residue from incomplete rinsing. Cornstarch or talc powders or medicated baby wipes are irritating the skin; switch to talc-free products and soap and water. Foods in the baby's or breastfeeding mother's diet are causing a change in the pH of the baby's urine. This change may be due to highly acidic foods like caffeine products (including chocolate), tomatoes, grapefruit, grapes, and sodas with citric acid. We recommend treating the rash with a zinc oxide, aloe vera, or calendula cream and exposing the area to fresh air as much as possible.

Biobottoms: This is a California-based company specializing in diaper covers. Classic **Biobottoms** are made of 100% fully felted, naturally absorbent wool. They keep clothes and bedding dry for about three to four diaper changes and can be machine washed and line dried. The velcro tummy panel makes it simple to take them off and put them on, and the added snaps for larger sizes keep babies from doing the same. They also produce **Cottonbottoms**, which are a completely waterproof option, with a cotton exterior and a smooth, impermeable polyester interior. These have the same hourglass design as **Biobottoms** and can be both machine washed and dried.

To go along with the covers, **Biobottoms** sells terry diapers with "thousands of thirsty loops" eagerly waiting to absorb whatever baby produces. These are 90% cotton woven with 10% polyester for extra durability (only the cotton touches baby's bottom). They can be folded in thirds and placed inside the diaper cover, or used with pins.

Price: Biobottoms are $13.50 each and come in five sizes. Expect to buy about twenty-five (five of each size) for the duration. They are available in cream, or cream with rainbow stitched edging, in regular or bikini style. **Cottonbottoms** are $10.50 and are available in yellow, blue, or cream. Terry diapers are $16/dozen in infant sizes and $22/dozen for toddlers. Choose pink or blue edging.

Happy Baby Bunz, a sixty-year-old California group, makes the **Nikky**, which is similar to wool **Biobottoms**, available in five sizes, with an inner leg binding to create a snug fit. They also make an all-cotton waterproof variety and cotton covers with vinyl waterproof lining.

Price: Wool covers are $10.75 each, ivory color only. Cotton waterproof are $9.50 each, and come in white with yellow, pink, or blue trim. Cotton print with vinyl liners are $6.50 each; they come in a yacht or shooting star print.

After the Stork, of Albuquerque, New Mexico, sells two models of cloth diapers, the pearl prefold and terry prefold. The pearl is an extra-soft 100% cotton with light blue trim, and the terries (the superabsorbents of the cloth set) are like small towels. This company also sells featherlite waterproof nylon pants, eliminating the brittle, tearable vinyl type. They are a significant savings over wool or cotton covers. Available in pull-on or snap styles.

Price: Pearl prefolds are $16.75/dozen. Terry prefolds are $19.95/dozen. Featherlites are $2.50–$3.25 each depending on size and style.

Pinless Diaper Pant: Produced by Sears and other companies, this variety has a waterproof nylon outer layer and a cotton blend inner lining, velcro closures, and elasticized leg openings. They come in four sizes but are not absorbent enough to use for nighttime diapering.

Price: A package of three for $8.99.

Standard Cotton Cloth: These are produced by department chains, like Sears and Penny's and also by Curity. The choice is birdseye or gauze weave. Birdseye is long wearing but less absorbent; gauze is softer and more absorbent. Both come in the prefold style, which is folded and sewn into baby shape, or flat, which can be folded to adjust to a growing body.

Price: Ranges from $8.99/dozen for flat birdseye to $16.99/dozen for heavyweight prefold gauze.

DI-D-Klips: These put an end to diaper pins. Rust-resistant stainless steel clips snap on and off with no sharp edges.

Price: $2/pair.

Warning: There have been documented cases of babies drowning in diaper pails. Get the buckets with locking lids and keep them in a child-proofed closet.

Note: Cloth diapers and the most expensive diaper covers, even with a diaper service, will save $500 to $800 over disposables. Plan on about $35 to $350 for diaper covers (nylon to wool) and another $100 for five dozen top-of-the-line terry diapers.

Best for Baby

Choosing diapers for your baby is an issue as personal as choosing underwear and as public as ecology. It's a matter of the family lifestyle, your cost, baby's comfort, and conscience. Our advice? We contend that the best thing for baby is no diaper at all, and the best thing for parents is potties.

Diaper Service—The Best of Both Worlds

The advent of disposables brought on a decline of the time-honored diaper service. Megabucks in advertising emphasized the dryness of disposables and overshadowed the other issues in diapering: bacteria, comfort, and waste disposal. As awareness grows about the potential hazards of throw-aways, diaper services around the country may make a comeback. They relieve parents (and their washing machines) of the delicate unpleasantries of diaper laundry and ensure the elimination of bacteria. Diapers are washed in 180-degree water, much hotter than in household machines. They are rinsed thoroughly to remove detergent residue and then often rinsed again with softeners and antiseptics for bacteria resistance. Plastic bags and a hamper are provided. Some services offer a choice of diaper styles—flat, prefolded, and with or without velcro closures. A fringe benefit: a cheerful pick-up and delivery person arrives on your doorstep weekly to comment on your baby's growth and remind new parents that the outside world of normal adults still exists.

Costs: About $10/week for five dozen diapers, half the price of keeping a baby in medium-sized disposables.

Best
Ointments **&** Lotions

*But let us hence, my
   sovereign, to provide
A salve for any sore that
   may betide.*

William Shakespeare

Best
Ointments
& Lotions

In the early colonial period, a minister was responsible for the physical as well as spiritual ills of his flock. It's heartening to know that while engrossed in the pursuits of passage to a better world, these men were not entirely above such mundane concerns as diaper rash. We have at least one recipe that comes down to us from the seventeenth century for a diaper rash salve. It includes hyssop, valerian, mercury, adder's tongue, yarrow, mellilot, and St. John's wort, and a note reminds us that it was good for other forms of skin irritation too. Another home remedy, this one from the midwest circa 1850, advises mixing the dried yellow centers of wild daisies with melted lard and applying it to the inflamed area.

The modern baby lotion business got underway in 1894 when a young company called Johnson & Johnson introduced a tin of pure talcum in a package called Simpson's Maternity Kit as an experiment. Mothers loved its moisture absorbing properties and soon the product was available simply as "Johnson's Powder."

Recently this benign substance talc has stirred quite a controversy. Two respected pediatricians published a study in the *American Journal of Diseases of Children*; it called for the removal of talc from the environment of children. Talc particles are not only miniscule (many cannot be seen with the usual optical microscope), they are flat (which is why talc feels so smooth). The particles, once ingested, cannot be removed by normal body mechanisms of elimination.

Isolated cases of excessive talc exposure have been linked to the onset of asthma in some children and at least one death (a child who was breathing through a tracheotomy tube). The media flurry that attended this attack revealed furthermore that talc was mined from the same mineral deposits as asbestos.

At this time the FDA has issued no bans on the use of talc in baby powder. Many companies still manufacture the old product but several now produce a cornstarch-based powder too. Since cornstarch has better absorption properties than talc anyway, we recommend using it exclusively.

Johnson & Johnson is still the industry giant. A number of other companies also produce excellent toiletries for infants. Below we list the major manufacturers and a few minor ones, their product(s), and a discussion of the ingredients used. We lean toward naturally produced products from natural ingredients. For example, sodium lauryl sulphate is the chemical name of a natural cleanser derived from coconuts. But seeing it listed among ingredients does not mean that it came from a coconut. A man-made synthesis, derived from petrochemicals, is widely used. If you would like more ingredient information, most pharmaceutical companies have a toll-free 800 number to call with inquiries.

Best for Baby

Johnson & Johnson

Baby Oil

This oil, invented in 1935, can be used as a cleanser, lubricant, and moisturizer. Its only ingredients are mineral oil and fragrance. Johnson & Johnson takes care to use only the highest quality oil that they then further filter themselves. Special considerations: Mineral oil has been identified as a potential carcinogen if ingested. Unlike some other oils which will penetrate the skin's surface, mineral oil sits on top, forming a moisture barrier. *Retail price: 8 oz./$1.29.*

Baby Powder Cornstarch

Cornstarch has wonderful natural absorption properties. (We would hate to be deprived of the nostalgic smell of childhood powder because of the dangers of talc). Johnson purifies their cornstarch well beyond the level required for regular food-grade cornstarch. Ingredients: 98% cornstarch, tricalcium phosphate, and fragrance. *Retail price: 4 oz./98¢.*

Baby Lotion

First introduced in 1944, this is a rich lotion with that famous baby fragrance. It is composed of a number of emollients to soften skin, humectants to help skin maintain moisture, and emulsifiers to make it easier to spread. Ingredients (listed in order of greatest concentration): water, propylene glycol, myristyl myristate, sodium stearate, glyceryl stearate, sodium oleate, polysorbate 61, isopropyl palmitate, sorbitan stearate, stearyl alcohol, beeswax, cetyl alcohol, carbomer-934, benzyl alcohol, methylparaben, propylparaben, butylparaben, BHT, fragrance, D & C Red #33. Special considerations: This ingredient list sounds daunting but most items are derivatives of naturally occurring elements, e.g., myristal myristate is the chemical name for a fatty acid found in nutmeg oil, coconut oil, etc. However, check with Johnson about the source, man-made or natural, by calling 1-800-526-3967. *Retail price: 4 oz./$1.89.*

Burroughs-Wellcome Company

Borofax

This hard-to-find ointment made its way into the marketplace in 1910. It works well for burns, abrasion, and chapping as well as your baby's skin. Ingredients: 5% boric acid (active), lanolin, fragrances, glycerin, mineral oil, purified water, and sodium borate. For information call 1-800-642-3194. *Retail: 1.75 oz./$4.39.*

Pfizer, Leeming Division

Desitin

This diaper rash ointment's claim to fame was the use of pure cod liver oil. Today it's still there although the primary ingredient is zinc oxide (recommended by some doctors by itself as a diaper rash antidote). Ingredients: Zinc oxide, butylated hydroxyaniscole, cod liver oil, fragrances, lanolin, methyparaben, white petrolatum, talc, purified water. Special considerations: The ointment does contain a small bit of talc, but it is mixed into the ointment and does not occur in powder form. We advise using it with discretion. If you have any further questions, call 1-800-352-3484. *Retail: 1 oz./$1.79.*

Autumn Harp

This is a natural cosmetics company with a small but excellent line of products designed for the baby. They responded quickly to the talc problem and created a baby powder made from pulverized herbs and blossoms. Again, they mix in small batches under immaculate conditions.

Earthchild Baby Powder

Has a pleasant, slightly medicinal smell. A good alternative to cornstarch if your baby is allergic. It can also be used by adults. Ingredients: Sago palm tree bark and trunk, calendula flowers (marigold), slippery elm bark, iris root, and natural flower oil essences for fragrance. *Retail: 3 oz./$3.25.*

Earthchild Baby Oil

Excellent for after bathing or for healing diaper rash. This product contains no petroleum derivatives, chemical preservatives, or synthetic fragrances. Ingredients: Olive oil, sweet almond oil, peanut oil, wheat germ oil (high in vitamin E and paba, a natural sunscreen), calendula flowers, comfrey leaves, mullein leaves, gum benzoin (a natural preservative), and natural flower fragrance. *Retail: 4 oz./$3.50.*

Comfrey Salve

The valuable healing powers of comfrey have been recognized since we began writing down recipes for medicines. It is excellent for cuts, bruises, bites, and stings as well as diaper rash. Ingredients: Olive oil, wheat germ oil, beeswax, comfrey leaves and roots, plantain leaves, goldenseal root, gum benzoin. *Retail: 1 oz./$3.75.*

Best for Baby

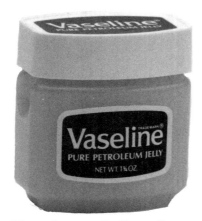

Chesebrough-Ponds

Vaseline Petroleum Jelly

This is pure, pharmaceutical-quality petrolatum jelly. The jelly is odorless and tasteless. It is frequently used as a cosmetic base or as a protective dressing for burns. Good for diaper rash too. For more information, call 1-800-243-5804. *Retail: 2 oz./89¢.*

Schering Corporation

A & D Ointment

This is often thought of for burns and scrapes, but it works well on babies' bottoms too. Ingredients: Sono Gel (petrolatum trade name), anhydrous lanolin, light mineral oil, fish liver oil, perfumes, cholecalciserol oil (vitamin D derivative). Their number is 1-800-526-4099. *Retail: 1.5 oz./$2.09.*

Weleda

Weleda is a fifty-year-old line of natural cosmetics and toiletries with a large following in Europe. They use only wild and organically grown herbs, plants, and flowers in preparing their products. They are mixed in small batches under immaculate conditions. Their baby line utilizes only unadulterated plant oils, beeswax, herbs, and calendula blossoms. We love these mild products, excellent for tender new skin, and recommend them.

Calendula Baby Oil

This oil will protect your baby's skin with a layer of warmth after bathing. Ingredients: Almond oil, calendula extract, chamomile extract, natural fragrance. *Retail: 2 fl. oz./$4.50.*

Calendula Baby Soap

This is one of the few soaps we came across formulated specifically for a baby's skin. It is extremely mild, lathers beautifully, and smells nice too. Ingredients: Calendula extract, palm oil, coconut oil, barley malt, chamomile extract, wild pansy herb, organic brown rice, iris rhisomes, natural fragrance. *Retail: $2.95 per bar.*

Calendula Baby Cream

This cream can be used as both a treatment and prevention for diaper rash. Ingredients: Peanut oil, water, beeswax, lanolin, cetearyl alcohol (an emulsifying wax) calendula extract, and natural fragrance. *Retail: 1.3 oz./$4.50.*

Best Mobiles

Best for Baby

*There was a child went
    forth each day
And the first object he
    look'd upon,
that object he became.*

Walt Whitman

Best Mobiles

The controversy about what infants can see goes back at least 100 years. Some said that children were color-blind (Charles Darwin was in this camp), and others insisted that they could see every color in the visible spectrum (which, when you vary brightness, hue, and saturation amounts to a grand total of 7.3 million colors). Some claimed that children could see color at 1 year, and others said not until age 6. The age/sequence theory held that the ability to perceive colors occurred one color at a time and in a predict-able sequence—first blue, then red, etc. Needless to say, all the experiments to prove these hypotheses had questionable validity.

Today, from well-orchestrated visual preference tests, we can give babies credit where credit is due. A newborn can see the parent that holds her and the breast or bottle that feeds her. Her range of vision extends about 7 to 12 inches, and some theorists believe that this is nature's built-in protection from a sensory overload caused by excessive visual stimulation. Newborns will blink their eyes to shield bright light, are sensitive to bright colors like red and yellow, and can detect contrasts of light and dark. A baby is selective in what she likes to look at and prefers human faces, patterns, sharp outlines and moving objects over stationary objects, plain surfaces, and solid forms.

By 1 month, an infant's range of vision is 7 to 18 inches. Eye-muscle coordination—the ability to focus both eyes on the same object—is developing and will be well established by 4 months. At this stage, a baby prefers bold, contrasting colors and light/dark patterns (like black and white) to pastels. The vestibular system of the inner ear, which governs the sense of balance, is stimulated by movement. This vestibular stimulation in turn affects eye movements. The combination of vestibular stimulation (any movement) and an upright position produces the most visual alertness in your baby; for example, holding your baby upright on your shoulder, supporting her head, and providing a gentle motion. This is probably why very young infants seem to have the clearest gaze while they're being held and rocked.

Infants 2 to 11 weeks old also have visual perception of danger. Studies were done of babies propped upright while objects hung with pulleys on a horizontal string moved toward them. When the object or its shadow appeared to be coming toward the infant on a collision course, she stiffened, moved her head, brought her arms to her face in defense, or whimpered. However, when the object was off to the side on a miss course, she just watched it move. This reaction requires swift perception of object/shadow direction and relative distance.

A 1 month old will fix her gaze on the outer edges of a face or shape. A baby is most interested in edges or boundaries and will stare at mother's hairline, rather than her smile. A 2 month old will scan and focus on facial features, provoking exclamations of, "She's looking at me! She knows me!"

By about 3 months, a baby's vision is almost equal to an adult's. The lenses of the eye adjust to a variety of focal lengths and a baby can perceive distance and depth. However, visual acuity—the sharpness of focus—is probably not as good as an adult's.

What I can see with my eyes, I point out with my finger.

Cervantes

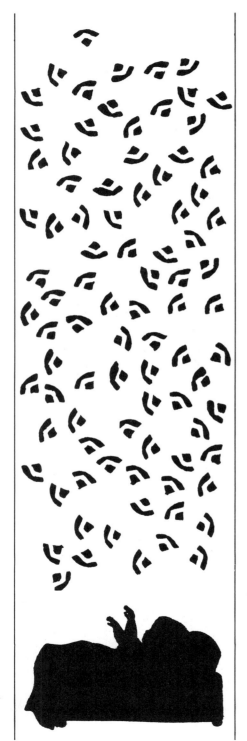

A baby is interested in a scene because of its meaning, movement, or shape. Once it's familiar, she'll become bored. But a slight variation, more than a dramatic one, will rekindle her interest. This indicates that a baby's attention is not random; she's comparing the slightly changed version with the one in her memory and forming concepts.

From a very young age babies have three-dimensional vision and can concentrate selectively. They're not at the mercy of the stimulation around them. By 2 months, they have visual-motor coordination and can bring an object they hear or feel next to them into their visual field. They respond selectively to color, preferring red and blue, and can divide colors into categories like blues, greens, etc. This early discrimination indicates that color classification is an innate ability and not acquired through learning the words for colors.

Mobiles are considered a terrific aid in the early stages of infant visual development, strengthening the ability to focus. They are equally useful later when a baby craves slight but detectable changes in the movement and shape of a visual object. A mobile can be made of plastic, vinyl, fabric, or even paper. Throughout your baby's first months, a mobile hung to the side rather than directly overhead will be easier for her to see. Make sure it is securely fastened and be careful to monitor your baby's growth, moving the mobile from the infant's reach before she tries to teeth on it or worse. Likewise, do not attach it to the crib unless it is specifically designed for such use.

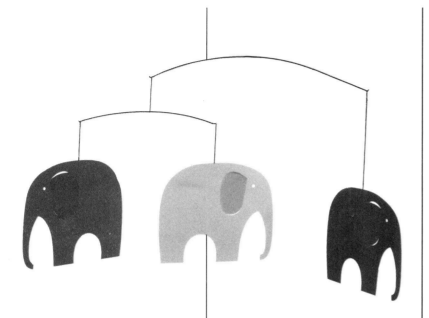

Voice-activated Mobile

Johnson & Johnson, the baby lotion giant, has recently developed a line of baby toys designed to enhance your child's development. Among these is the world's first **Voice-activated Mobile** especially for infants. The sound of a baby's voice (and miniaturized microchip technology) makes the mobile play "Twinkle, Twinkle, Little Star" for three minutes. The mechanism can also be shut off. The four soft vinyl stars have been designed to face downward. The mobile can be affixed to the crib until a baby is 5 months, at which time the manufacturer recommends moving it to a wall. *Price: $29.95.*

Elephant Party

Elephant Party is a mobile produced in Denmark by Flemstead Mobiles and sold through the Museum of Modern Art. Three paper-thin plastic elephants in red, blue, and yellow float lazily in the air. **Elephant Party's** clean, sharp lines and strong colors will appeal to your baby during the first 2 months. The subtle visual play created by the fold-out ears will entertain thereafter. We like it near a strong light source that produces shadows. Its simplicity makes it a nice mobile for more contemporary nurseries. *Available through the Museum's catalog for $10.*

Best *for* **B**aby

Bright Baby Mobile

Bright Baby Mobile is part of the state-of-the-art infant development system called Blanc & Noir designed by Dr. Susan Luddington-Hoe (co-author of *How to Have a Smarter Baby*). This system of objects is intended to stimulate babies in their first important year. The mobile is made of soft black and white vinyl decorated in the variegated patterns older babies love and the circle patterns preferred by newborns. The mobile is attached to a plastic arm that fastens on the crib rail. Available exclusively through F.A.O. Schwarz and their catalog. *Approximate retail: $50.*

Clowning Around

Clowning Around is the best-selling baby mobile in the United States. Five plush toy clowns, again cleverly faced downward to suit a baby's perspective, frolic with balloons. They are dressed in red, blue, yellow, and green and have clearly drawn pattern faces surrounded by orange hair. The mobile winds up and plays Shubert's Lullaby. As a baby grows older, the clowns can be cut loose and used as toys. **Clowning Around** also comes with an armature that can be attached to a crib rail. *Approximate retail: $45 to $50.*

Best Toys

Best for Baby

*I will make brooches and
toys for your delight
Of birdsong at morning
and starshine at night.*

Robert Louis Stevenson

Best Toys

The Egyptians made some of the earliest toys extant. Their children played with dolls, tops, and pull-along animals. Painted cows seem to have been especially popular. The presence of many toys in the sarcophagi of children has lead archeologists to speculate that these toys had the double purpose of warding off evil.

Although studies have shown that similar toys are popular the world over, they also reflect the character of the culture in which they were made. Ancient Greek toys place a strong emphasis on physical skills and endurance. Their dolls had joints for movement. Toys that involved physical activity, like hoops, were frequently depicted on the sides of Greek vases.

From medieval times, very few examples survive. Historians attribute this lack to all the sacking and pillaging that occurred. Judging from woodcuts of the day, hobby horses and whirligigs were most common. There are records of various noble children receiving gifts of toy cannons and the like, probably to help them imagine the rather bellicose lifestyle that lay ahead.

We do not see an abundance of toys again until the Renaissance. Rather than an explosion of toys, we see a slow but steady increase of number and type. Toys from this era tended to be solid and educational in nature. By contrast, toys for grown-ups, making their first appearance, captured the fanciful imagination of toymakers; elaborate dollhouses were the vogue.

In eighteenth-century America, toys for the rich were primarily imported from Europe. In this period, people began to cater to the needs and tastes of their children. A rocking horse with wheels appeared many places in the colonies, and puppets were popular. Noah's Ark was common among Puritans, largely because it was the only toy permissible on the Sabbath. Paper dolls modeled on popular ballerinas and singers gained a foothold and also served as a way to spread the new fashions.

In the nineteenth century, the industrial revolution brought about the first mass production of toys, but an interest in painstaking craftsmanship still prevailed. Moveable dolls were standard. The first speaking doll was invented in 1820. It said mama if you lifted its right arm and papa if you lifted its left. Mechanical toys and music boxes appeared in quantity. Wooden toys from the workshops of Germany were world famous.

The twentieth century saw the introduction of the teddy bear named after Teddy Roosevelt and the first electric trains that actually worked. Toy airplanes took off shortly after the Wright Brothers historic flight. This century has been characterized by the politicizing of toys. Toy soldiers were popular around World War I. This period also saw the first public

Best for Baby

outcry against violent toys, and the movement gained steam in the twenties. A general ban on German toys prevailed in this country after the war. This ban in turn set the American toy boom in motion.

In the past thirty years a trend to design toys for very specific stages of childhood development has appeared. Many child specialists now suggest that toys be as free from detail as possible to stimulate a child's imagination. Versatile toys with two or more functions give a toddler a greater sense of the power he has over his environment. The best and most favored toys are large and easily manipulated. Finally, toys that encourage cooperation rather than aggression are recommended.

When purchasing a toy for your child, you should make sure that it is well-made with no sharp edges or points to hurt him. All toy enamels or sealants are federally regulated to be lead-free and nontoxic but check anyway. A toy should be shatterproof and easily cleaned. Stay away from battery-operated or electrical toys until your child is about 6, and check all toys frequently for damage that could endanger your child.

There is a wide array of toys to choose from today. In assembling the following selection, we have tried to include the classics of infancy and childhood, the toys almost no child goes without. Some are new twists on old themes (like the Gloucester Rocker), and others are identical to the same toy used hundreds of years ago (the plain wooden blocks). We have chosen them for their uniformly high quality and safety. They have been grouped according to age, but this is only a general guideline. Your baby's individual development should be considered.

0 to 9 Months

A Rattle

In many civilizations, a baby's first toy has been a rattle. The one you see here is carved by Elwood Turner of Morrisville, Vermont from a single piece of rock maple. This is a particularly strong hardwood. The shaft is thick and unbreakable, and the 1 9/16 inch rattle end meets Consumer Product Safety standards to prevent infant choking. The rattle comes unfinished, making it safer for baby to chew on. Rock maple is the most chemically pure hardwood available. The wood also makes a lovely clacking sound. The rattle can be used by infants as young as 3 months, but we recommend waiting until baby is about a half year old. *Approximate retail: $11 to $13.*

Tender Teddy

Where would childhood be without a teddy? **Tender Teddy** by Gund is especially nice for tiny babes because of his small size. Whatever stuffed animal you choose, remember to check that the animal has safety lock eyes (to frustrate older prying fingers) and a short pile that doesn't pull out easily. Your teddy should be both machine washable and driable. It's especially important to remove all bows, ribbons, or anything else your baby could possibly chew on. It's also nice, if not absolutely necessary, that your stuffed toy be baby-sized. *Approximate retail: $12.*

Bright Baby Tactile Tillie

Another item from the Blanc & Noir line from France (see the mobile on page 66), **Bright Baby Tactile Tillie** is made from nine fabrics with nine textures. She is designed to stimulate baby's sense of touch as he runs his hand along the cotton, burlap, satin, and so forth. Several fabrics also feature the black and white patterns that infants love and that help in vision development. Tillie is imported exclusively by F.A.O. Schwarz. *Approximate retail: $45.*

9 to 24 Months

Animal Sound Barn

At about 9 months, baby will become fascinated by sound. A perennial favorite for encouraging this development is **Animal Sound Barn** by Fisher-Price. It contains five different animal sounds and lots of push and pull action. By coupling sight and sound—pull the bone and hear the dog bark, squeeze the duck and hear her quack— conceptual development is stimulated. Infants will be entertained up to age 3. *Approximate retail: $11.50.*

Car Seat Circus

If your child is fidgety, we recommend the **Car Seat Circus** by Summer. Three soft plastic toys stimulate eye-hand coordination, finger dexterity, and tactile sensitivity. The elephant squeaks and has a soft vinyl ring on the end of its trunk for teething. The clown's juggling hoops push from side to side. The bear's barbells bounce and clack, and he answers back. Attaches easily to all types of car seats with Velcro fasteners. *Approximate retail: $15.*

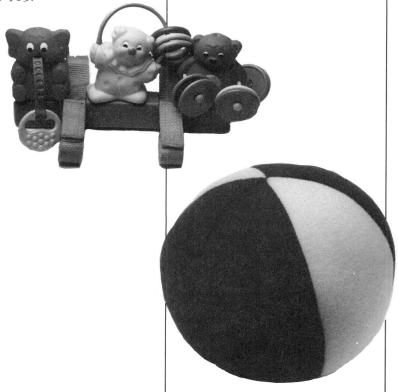

Large Rattle Ball

This large rattle ball is made by Battat. The bright and colorful ball rattles when shaken or tossed. It is covered in soft, machine-washable fabric. Good for infants from 5 or 6 months and up. Also available in a smaller size. *Approximate retail: $8.*

Turtle Sandbox

At about 18 months, most children are ready to play with sand. At that time, we recommend **Turtle Sandbox** by Little Tikes. The heavy-duty green plastic construction has no parts to rust. Turtle's "shell" swings off easily at playtime and swings back on after, keeping sand safe from weather and pets who may choose it for a litter box. The color won't fade and the plastic is chip-resistant. The sandbox weighs only 23 pounds. *Approximate retail: $40.*

Paddleboat

This popular toy manufactured by the Woodworks Toy Company of Oregon (whose owner proudly proclaims to be "one of the smallest toy companies in the U.S.") is based on an early American folk toy. The solid hardwood boat is powered by a rubber band. The paddlewheel and person are stained a darker color for contrast. Perfect for bathtub or beach, this will stimulate 18-month-old mechanical engineers everywhere. The finishing oil is nontoxic when dried and cured. *Approximate retail: $5.75*

Gentle Mouse Bouncer

Part furniture and part toy, this **Gentle Mouse Bouncer** made from a large piece of foam is a new concept designed to be used by infants on up. The toy is adaptable to a number of uses, challenging a baby's imagination as he grows older. First Step, the manufacturer, uses only the highest quality fabrics and flame-retardant foam. Each piece is first covered in a 100% nylon sheath, then recovered in 100% cotton, which is removable and washable. An added plus: **Gentle Mouse** will never pinch fingers the way a more traditional riding toy may. The company produces a number of different bouncing animals, in a wide variety of colors. *Approximate retail: $58.*

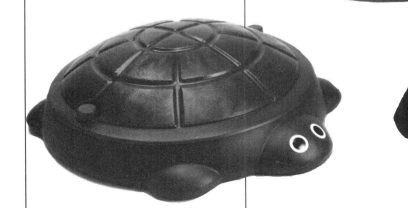

Original Gloucester Rocker

This exquisite toy, the nautical answer to the rocking horse, was originally designed by a man named Buckley Smith for his own child. It is based on the classic lines of a Gloucester fishing dory, used for centuries off the New England coast. The rocker is handmade using mahogany and pine and comes in blue or green with a red waterline, or red with blue waterline. An imposter was recently spotted near these shores, so make sure your rocker comes with the **Original Gloucester Rocker** numbered brass plaque affixed to the transom. Guaranteed to weather most childhood storms, the 3-foot-long rocker can be used by your baby from age 2 onward and with adult supervision even earlier than that. *Approximate retail: $275. Note:* A limited hand-made collector's edition is also available for about $100 more.

Block Crayons

The Stockmar Company of West Germany makes a line of art materials from the finest nontoxic ingredients. They produce a wonderful set of richly colored block crayons, perfect even for 1-year-old hands. All their products are mixed in small, quality-controlled batches. They are used to the exclusion of all others by Waldorf Schools (see School section) around the world. We can't recommend them enough. A set of sixteen in a lovely tin box will cost you *approximately $9.80.*

Truth's Baby Doll

It's hard to choose a doll. So many terrific ones are made. When forced to choose, however, we came up with **Truth's Baby Doll.** She (or he) is handmade from natural materials chosen for their beauty, texture, and durability. The body is covered in a flesh-toned cotton knit. The hair is a wool-mohair blend. The dolls are filled with 100% woolen fleece to just the right point, so that they are firm but flexible. The simple, abstract faces allow your baby to better imagine it as herself, which is what she is doing in large part when doll playing anyway. *Retail price: $48.*

Bright Blocks

Bright Blocks are a lego-type toy but larger and easier to manipulate. They come in various sizes in a range of primaries or pastels. The company just introduced a mottled gray version for castle-building. The high-density plastic is flexible but cannot be shattered. The corners of all Bright Blocks are rounded and the surfaces are textured for safety. The snap-together knobs are uniform so all blocks, no matter what size, will fit each other. This is an excellent block for ages 18 months onward. Available in a six-block Sampler right on up to the Castlemaster with 257 pieces. A Starter set with six-teen blocks *retails for approx-imately $13*.

36 Months and Up

My Train

My Train is a nifty hand-powered version especially suitable for toddlers. It is built to stand up to very energetic play. In fact, their producer, Montgomery Schoolhouse, guarantees them without time limit (and will repair one for free should it break). There are nine different cars to choose from, plus engine and caboose. The one here features a log carrier with removable logs, a car carrier, and a crane car with a crane that can be played with separately. **My Train** is painted with an array of brightly colored, nontoxic enamels. Recommended for age 3 and up. *Approximate retail: $50*.

Wooden Blocks

A beautifully made, classic set of hardwood maple wooden blocks can be obtained from Community Playthings out of Rifton, New York. The set for 3 year olds contains thirty-two blocks in seven shapes. All blocks are left in their unvarnished state and can be cleaned with soap and water. *Note:* This group also manufactures a large line of toys for disabled children. See address information under Some Wonderful Toy Catalogs at the end of this section. *Retail price for the 3-year-old set: $38.75*.

Best for Baby

The Kindercolor Express

This is a three-dimensional maze made of five separate wires in a hardwood base. The wires are strung with wooden beads in a variety of shapes and bright colors. It helps young children recognize color, sizes, shapes, and numbers. They develop their visual and motor skills, while having plain old-fashioned fun. This is a durable toy with no rough surfaces or sharp edges, and the mobile parts cannot be removed. Highly recommended. *Approximate retail: $50–$70.*

Omagles

Omagles are a new modular plastic building toy by Gerber. Precision-molded bright yellow pipes are connected by a variety of hinges and locking clips. They are easy for small hands to manipulate and can be built into cars, secret hiding places, or whatever your child dreams up. Good for ages 3 and up. The Motion-Maker Set comes with 120 pieces. *Approximate retail: $120.*

For Parents

Playcraft Bookcase With Cubbies

This is a another child-safe toy organizer with moms and dads in mind. It is made of a durable but extremely lightweight molded plastic. The cubbies remove easily and can be stacked—no heavy toy chest lids to fall on children's heads. As your child grows older, the cubbies can be removed to make a bookcase. The unit comes in light blue or rose with off-white shelves. Matching cubbies are available. *Approximate retail: Bookcase $29 to $35. Cubbies are $7 to $9 each.*

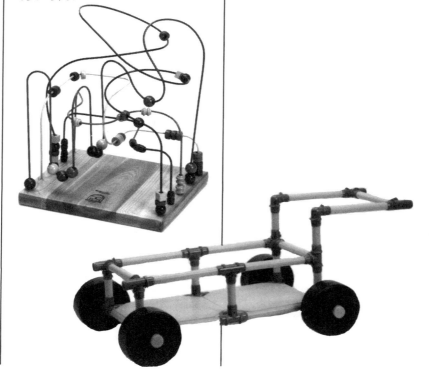

Tyke Hike

Tyke Hike is a collapsible mesh toy box. The metal frame is a bright powder-coated aluminum. The toy box is portable, lightweight, and waterproof. It comes in a combination of primary colors. *Approximate retail: $40.*

Some Wonderful Toy Catalogs

Community Playthings
Route 213
Rifton, New York 12471

Great wooden gym equipment and child furniture. A good selection of multicultural dolls. They also have a separate catalog especially for disabled children's toys and aids.

Constructive Playthings
Call 1-800-255-6124 or in Missouri 1-816-761-5900 for a free catalog.

A good selection from a number of top manufacturers. They also have anatomically correct dolls. One popular toilet-training book suggests using them to help teach your child, but the boy dolls are hard to find.

Educational Teaching Aids
199 Carpenter Avenue
Wheeling, IL 60090

This is the consumer's version of a catalog used widely by schools. Great toys and play equipment classified by category like Role Playing, Perceptual Manipulatives, and so on.

Hearth Song
P.O. Box B
Sebastopol, CA 95473
(707) 829-1550

Fabulous wooden toys, dolls, art supplies, and educational play things.

Violent Toys

Currently five of the top six best-selling toys are war-related. Parents often blithely excuse such toys as a "useful means of letting out aggression" or a "good catharsis" to help a child get rid of anger in a constructive way. But recent studies indicate that acting out aggression via violent toys or any other method rather than relieving a situation makes the aggressive feeling worse. Dr. Charles Turner at the University of Utah conducted a study of two groups of preschoolers: those playing with toys, and those playing with toys including guns. He observed that in the second group, even if the children did not actually play with the guns, their mere presence increased antisocial physical and verbal behavior. Another study of college-age students revealed a similar disturbing result. The study concerned itself with a booth at a campus carnival where people threw sponges at a clown. A significantly greater number of sponges were thrown when a rifle was nonchalantly placed to one side of the booth than when the rifle was absent. Still other studies have made clear links between violent behavior and violence on TV. Even Sylvester Stallone is on record saying that he won't let his own children play with a Rambo doll. The message seems clear: If you want a more peaceful world and a more peaceful child in it, avoid these toys. If your child insists, make him pay for them himself.

For an excellent list of age-appropriate and nonviolent toys, send a SASE and 25 cents to:

Toys: Tools for Learning
National Association for the Education
    of Young Children
1834 Connecticut Avenue NW
Washington, D.C. 20009

Best Clothing

Best for Baby

*Had I the heavens' embroidered cloths,
Enwrought with gold and
silver light.*

W. B. Yeats

Proper Care of
Infant Clothing

Care of your baby's new clothing is very simple. Before first use, all indoor wear including diapers should be put through a wash cycle without soap or detergent to get rid of sizing. From then on launder all items in soap flakes like Dreft. Do not use detergents, which leave residues harmful to new skin. For flame-retardant items that cannot be washed in soap, use only a small amount of detergent and put the item through two rinse cycles.

Best
Clothing

The seventeenth century marks the beginning of children's *fashions* as opposed to mere functional clothing. Styles reflected the attitude that children were small adults. Boys and girls dressed like men and women, who in turn dressed remarkably like each other. This period is characterized by a taste for jewels, rich fabric, and decoration to excess.

For the next three centuries, dressing a child as a small adult continued. Occasionally youthful clothing broke from this mold and ranged ahead or behind the times. Hanging sleeves, an ornamental extra pair seen on the clothing of the rich in both Europe and China for almost 200 years, disappeared from everything but infant frocks in the late seventeenth century. On the other hand, during the eighteenth century trousers appeared on older boy children a good fifty years ahead of men, who were still wearing breeches. During this same period, yellow, not white, was the traditional color of christening clothes. For day-to-day clothing, infants were wrapped tightly in swaddling clothes that often doubled as diapers.

During the nineteenth century, although children's clothes were simpler than their adult counterparts, they were still hopelessly impractical for play. It was not until the twentieth century that fashions changed. Children's clothes began to be designed for children. Girls took to wearing the more practical bloomers, instead of petticoats. Boys, who were dressed identically to girls until around age 5, began to be dressed like boys from birth. Styles for both grew shorter and shorter. It's interesting that this growing awareness of the peculiar clothing requirements of childhood paralleled an increasing recognition of the child as quite different from the adult. Only for dress-up did styles hold to earlier custom. The thirties saw tiny Chanel suits for girls and Eton suits for boys, replicas of mom and dad.

What happens in clothing and fashion reflects what is happening in the world. In the past forty years, kids clothes have become increasingly less constraining and more sport- and play-oriented. It's no wonder in our youth-obsessed culture that today adults take the lead from children's styles and appear in kidlike clothing. It may not be a bad change.

The fabric of choice for infant clothing, especially next to skin, is cotton. Clothing should be loose-fitting with no tight collars or cuffs. It should be roomy enough around the bottom to easily cover diapers. The better-made infant garments also have double-sewn seams to avoid irritation.

During the 1950s, the Flammable Fabrics Act was passed. It introduced strict standards for infant sleepware. Unfortunately, these standards resulted in the widespread use of flame-resistant chemical finishes like TRIS that were later found to be extremely carcinogenic. Today chemical finishes to retard flammability have mostly disappeared, but it is still better to use nightwear made from an inherently flame-retardant synthetic fabric rather than a fabric to which flame-retardant chemicals have been added. More and more parents we talk to simply put their infants to sleep in cotton playwear, but this is a decision that must be made individually. The most naturally flame-retardant natural fibers were wool and particularly silk. Cotton itself is highly flammable. Whatever your choice, the most sensible thing to do is keep small children well away from open hearths and matches that cause most of the accidents in the first place.

With regard for the increasing number of double career families who haven't the time to shop for clothing, we have organized our clothing section around top-quality children's wear catalogs. To begin, however, we review a few of the children's styles that have become modern classics. They are generally for fancy occasions.

Shoes for Toddlers

Experts and retailers agree that crib shoes (those worn before a child's feet bear weight) are not necessary. But they're cute and can keep feet warm.

When a child's feet begin to bear weight, they need shoes. Early shoes should provide protection, balance, and style. They range from supportive (high-top leather shoes) to flexible (soft-soled lightweight types). See After the Stork section. Today many people prefer the latter. The foot needs to be free to bend and exercise its muscles, and soft shoes promote this requisite flexibility. If you do purchase high-top shoes, make sure they have soft uppers for freedom of movement and breathability. Toddler shoes should have also have a broad front so toes can move and spread. Antislip soles for this age are a nice plus. Make sure there are no hard or constricting supports inside your baby's shoe either. Exercise, not a bump, creates a strong arch.

When you visit a shoe store, have the salesperson fit both feet. One foot is usually larger than the other. A proper fit should leave about half an inch of toe room on the larger foot. Also, do not pass toddler shoes on. Shoes mold to one child and can cause awkwardness and discomfort for the next.

For indoor use, a new option for toddling feet is socks with rubberized soles. Look for this new footwear in clothing stores.

Best for Baby

Florence Eiseman

Florence Eiseman began designing and making clothes in 1932 for her own children and those of friends. Thirteen years later, when she began selling her styles to the public, she made fashion history. A Florence Eiseman dress was not quite like anything on the market. They were simple A-line designs made from bright colors and the finest materials. Her signature was a simple appliqué on each garment. Mothers loved them because they could be passed down without looking tired or worn. A friend of ours remembers wearing a *second generation* Eiseman original.

Today the business remains a family operation committed to high quality. They have eliminated things like French seams to help keep prices down. An Eiseman crea-tion has the reputation of being high-priced, but some retailers we talked to said this was fallacious. For dress-up you won't find better quality at a better price. Dresses range from $25 to $110. They have a full line of boys clothes in sizes 6 months to 6X. Girls styles go up to size 14. *Approximate retail: Jumper/$50. Shirt/$14. Puffed Sleeves Dress/$75.*

Rothchild & Company

Rothchild is the oldest manufacturer of outerwear for children in the country. Their first coat dates back to 1881. Today their coats are made with the same high quality that has kept them in business so long. Their most popular style for boys is the double-breasted Navy Regulation coat with brass anchor buttons, a nautical emblem on the left sleeve and a matching cap. For girls we like this red wool melton coat with navy piping and shawl collar. The main seam on a Rothchild coat is in back instead of along the sides, allowing the coat to hang more easily on active children. The coats are also fully lined. Many winter styles have matching leggings. Prices range from $70 to $150. *The Navy Regulation you see here is $80. The girl's coat is $110.* Both in toddler sizes.

The Laura Ashley Mother & Child Collection

This new line of children's and infant's clothing features the same quality and work-manship that women every-where have come to expect from the Laura Ashley organi-zation. The designs tend heav-ily toward the upper class English country look, a world of prams and Norland nannies. The styles are primarily for fancy occasions and come in a range of Laura Ashley fabrics. After seeing these lovely, well-made garments, we wondered why they hadn't done this years ago. Baby's clothing is in the $10 to $40 range. Girls dresses go up to $72. *The Unisex Romper featured here is $68 to $72 depending on size.*

The John-John Suit

Imp originals had been making their short-all or jump-short for almost twenty years when it was made world famous by John Kennedy, Jr. scampering about the White House. Today, more than twenty-five years after that, the John-John is still one of their top sellers. The suit is made year round in a variety of fabrics appropriate to the season. For spring there are linens, twills, and seersuckers. For fall you can choose among corduroy, solid flannels, tartan plaids, and, for dressier occa-sions, velveteen. The Eton-collared cotton shirt is sold separately. *Approximate retail: In linen $20. In tartan plaid wool blend $24. Shirt $12.*

The Smocked Dress

Smocking is one of those processes that machines haven't made better. For a source of top-quality hand-smocked dresses we suggest Nantucket Designs. Denny Buckley, who started the company, had plenty of expo-sure to cottage industries during her six-year stay in Nepal. Back in this country and looking for something to support herself during the Nan-tucket winters, she began to design and sell hand-smocked dresses. The dresses are available in a wide variety of fabrics for ages 6 months to preteens. She also makes quilts and day gowns for infants. Prices for the dresses range from $60 to $180 depending on fabric and smocking pattern. *The exam-ples here sell for $140 and $150.*

Best for Baby

Great Children's Clothing Catalogs

Les Petits

Les Petits is a chain of thirteen children's clothing stores in France. In this country their clothing is available only by catalog. This line is a bit more fashion-conscious than any of the others featured here, but they don't go overboard. Designs are simple with small details adding the twist. They carry polos in nine remarkable jewel-like colors for infants on up. They have an outstanding selection of floral print dresses with exquisite collars at good prices. Where else can you find children's hand-made, ribbon-laced espadrilles in this country? A catalog is free for asking by calling 1-800-225-1158.

Hanna Anderson

All Hanna's clothing is 100% cotton. She primarily carries knit playwear—t-shirts, sweats, rompers, stretchies, etc.—in a range of solids or stripes. The garments are made with 100% cotton thread. Seams are flat double sewn so as not to irritate tender skin. The clothes are full-cut to allow for diapers and active play. Every piece comes with a name tag. The collars and cuffs are rib-knit so that you may order extra-large and have your child grow into the garment.

Sizing is by height to give a better fit. Hanna also has an innovative program called Hanna-downs. Any clothing that has seen the use of only one child and is returned to them in good used condition will be given a 20% catalog credit. Hanna donates the clothing to worthy causes for you. This is a fine company with an excellent product. They have a few styles available in parent sizes too. To order a free catalog call 1-800-222-0544.

After the Stork

After the Stork was a pioneer just seven years ago in introducing only 100% cotton clothing in their line. They are a dedicated group who work hard to keep their prices down. In truth, prices are the best we've come across. The company originated with Pedi-Bares, a soft leather infant moccasin with special lacing that allows an infant's foot to grow one full size. Today their line is largely based on rugged, functional separates in bright colors. They feature silk-screened sweatshirts, school-quality sweats, and corduroy jumpers among other things. They have a good selection of cotton underwear too. Nikky diaper covers (see page 52) are available. Call (505) 243-9100 for a free catalog.

Garnet Hill

Although Garnet Hill does not specialize in children's clothes, they have an excellent small selection. They carry Nikky diaper covers, swiss cotton toddler underwear, and Absorba layette pieces among other items. An excellent source for wool and cotton maternity tights and flannel crib sheets too. The company's emphasis is on natural fiber products in general. We don't think you'll be disappointed if you call 1-800-622-6216 for a free catalog.

Biobottoms

Biobottoms, makers of the breathable diaper covers described on page 52, offers a wonderful catalog of natural fiber children's wear as well. They carry primarily play-clothes in classic styles. They also have a nice selection of shoes and some innovative toys and furniture. Biobottoms features a great line of velours. Prices are reasonable too. For a free catalog, please call (707) 778-7945.

Best for Baby

Patagonia

Some of the world's best-made and most thoughtfully designed outerwear and sports clothing for adults is made by this twelve-year-old California firm. Three years ago, they decided to extend this expertise to a small line of rugged kids' clothes, inspired by a number of employees who were having babies. The catalog is published twice a year. No dresses to be had here. The line is limited to pants, shorts, shirts, and outerwear in synchilla (a fabric designed for adult expeditions to the Arctic) or shelled synchilla primarily. Hip kidlike colors are a company trademark. This is a catalog even adults fight over when it first arrives. You'll thank your kid forever. Call 1-800-523-9597 for a free one. In California it's 1-800-432-0241.

Brights Creek

Brights Creek is the largest children's specialty wear catalog in the United States. They carry adorable infant sweats, regulation sleepwear, ribbed cotton-knit cardigan/skirt/legging outfits. They also have a good selection of Soupcon and lovely pastel layette items. Although they carry a number of different manufacturers, every item is made to their own specifications and is exclusive to them. The items in the catalog are an excellent value for the money. To be put on their mailing list call 1-800-622-9202.

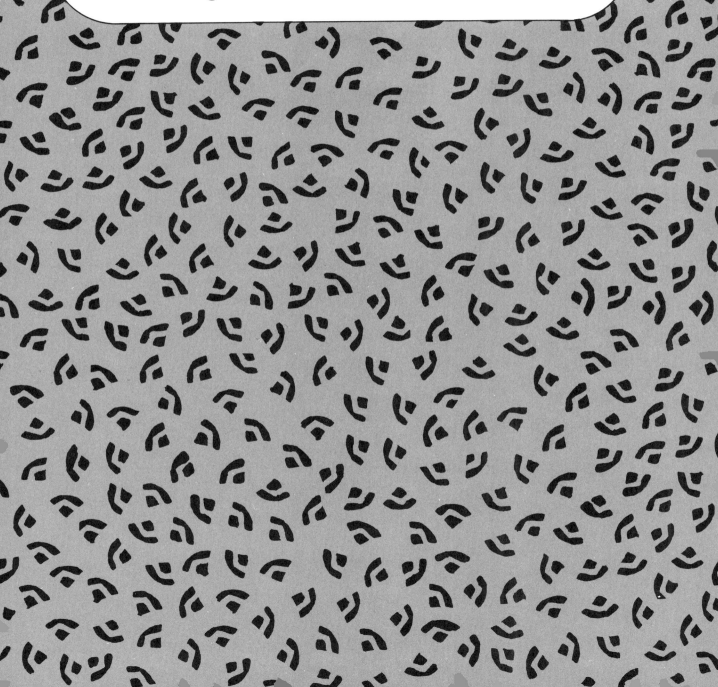

Best
Baby Food **&** Diet

*I have given suck, and know
How tender 'tis to love the
babe that milks me.*

William Shakespeare

Best Baby Food & Diet

Whether or not to breastfeed is a question that even a nineteenth-century woman faced. It wasn't fashionable to offer mother's milk, but there were no cans of ready-to-feed formula on supermarket shelves. The alternative was a wet nurse— a woman hired to breastfeed your baby. Her qualifications had to be more than just an abundant milk supply; the crucial factor was her hair color.

It was popular belief that hair color reflected temperament, and that a baby inherited the disposition of the woman who nursed her. Brunettes were said to be the most stable and have the strongest physical and emotional make-up; hence, the best milk. The supposed tendency toward melancholia in these darker women ensured heavier milk that prevented too much mental excitement in babies, which could interfere with physical development. Blondes were typed as too passionate. The heat of their passion made their milk deteriorate, and in some cases, experts concluded, the milk of blondes caused infant deaths. Of course, out of the question were red-headed wet nurses, who were prone to irritability and fits of temper and could possibly encourage criminal tendencies in a child.

Late in the century, infant food companies introduced an alternative to nursing. From the 1870s to the 1940s, these companies developed feeding formulas. By the fifties, they had a mutually advantageous relationship with the medical profession; new mothers were handed the infant on one arm and formula in the other.

These powdered formulas were a marvelous improvement over their homemade counterparts. Women had been diluting evaporated milk with water to decrease the concentration of cow's milk proteins (too high for a baby to digest), and adding sugar to compensate for the necessary lactose lost in the dilution. It was common for pediatricians to see infants who were quite ill from too much or too little dilution, from contamination during preparation and bottling, and from salt mistakenly used instead of sugar.

With breastfeeding so convenient, why were women working so hard to find alternatives? It seems to boil down to trends. The urban woman was the rage—chic, up-to-date, and on-the-go. Women were afraid of what nursing might do to their figures and were convinced that they'd be freer to clean the house and care for their other offspring if baby got used to a bottle. Certainly, women who worked outside the home needed at least a supplement to the breast.

When powdered formulas hit the market in the fifties and sixties most women couldn't resist them. These innovations were supplied by manufacturers to hospitals (often free), and hospitals passed these free samples onto new mothers. Women who wanted to breastfeed commonly saw nurses weigh their babies before and after each nursing to see if the infant had gotten enough milk. Such practices made mothers so anxious that they were often discouraged from breastfeeding and opted for the certainty of the bottle. By 1979, the *Pediatric Nutrition Handbook* written by the American Academy of Pediatrics devoted two pages to breastfeeding and fifteen pages to the bottle. Rumor has it, the Soviets called us Americans "milkless women."

Ask your child what he wants for dinner only if he is buying.

Fran Leibowitz

Best for Baby

Meanwhile, formula manufacturers looked to science to upgrade the nutritional value of their mixtures, making them even more desirable to consumers. The model for this improved mixture of minerals, protein, and carbohydrates, just suited for baby, was breast milk. As this regard for breast milk became widely known, women began to think the obvious, "If my milk is perfect for my baby, why not breastfeed?"

The growing concern in the late seventies over food additives prompted many to reject packaged foods. This return to au natural as the theme for healthy living encouraged more and more women to nurse their newborns. Publicity about formulas improperly marketed in Third World Countries that caused infant deaths stirred public awareness about the lack of corporate conscience. Ill-feelings about formula and its manufacturers grew.

The emotional rewards of breastfeeding, as well as new research on the inimitable superiority of mother's milk, heralded a return to breastfeeding in the eighties. Today twice as many women breastfeed as did ten years ago, and almost four times as many are still nursing three months later.

Human milk is a complete source for the nutrition of a baby for the first six months (some say first year) of life. It has an ideal combination of protein, carbohydrates, fats, minerals, and most vitamins with two to ten times the essential vitamins as unfortified

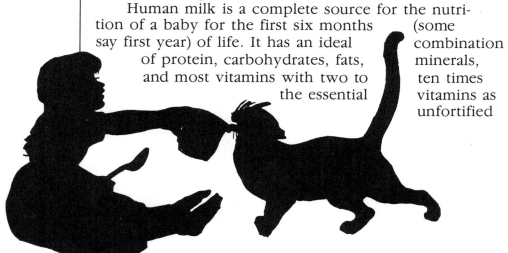

cow's milk. This difference is doubled once the cow variety is diluted. Human milk is low in vitamins A, D, and C, and some physicians recommend vitamin supplements for these nutrients (see sidebar). Although the iron content of breast milk is low, it's absorbed better than the iron from cow's milk. Some nutritionists say human milk contains two proteins that protect infants from infectious bacteria, and these proteins can't work in the presence of too much iron.

Recently, the studies about the relationship between breast milk and reduced infection have been questioned, but the American Academy of Pediatrics still maintains that breast milk is nutritionally superior to formula for fat, cholesterols, protein, and iron. Human milk also simulates cells to divide and produce enzymes that aid digestion. It stimulates the maturation of the intestinal tract, which helps baby to be more food tolerant.

Formulas are a delicate and complicated balance of nutrients, mimicking the composition of human milk. Although they lack some of the elusive growth factors of breast milk, they are perfectly adequate, total nutritional sources for a baby's first six months. Most formulas use cow's milk as their base. The milk is skimmed and then diluted to decrease the amount of proteins and minerals that a baby can't digest. Vegetable oils are added to replace the fat in cow's milk, and some form of sugar (preferably lactose which is milk sugar) is added to equal the levels in breast milk.

Some formulas are a combination of cow's milk and demineralized whey milk that better simulates the amount of protein and minerals in human milk. There are also soy-based formulas for babies who are allergic to the protein or lactose in cow's milk. However, soy protein is harder for a baby to digest, so cow's milk formulas should be your first choice.

Gerber or gourmet, mealtimes should be fun for a baby—an adventure in taste and texture, not a battle of wills. Normal babies won't starve themselves and need time to adjust to each new food. When your baby starts to reach for food, smack his or her lips, meditate on the motion of your fork, or do imitations of you in the act, he or she is ready for the first mouthful.

Baby's Garden

This new California line bills as all natural but the products are not necessarily organically grown. You can be sure, however, that they won't put in any additives, sugars, or modified starches. Baby's Garden is packaged aseptically; the plastic containers are sterilized first and then filled. This line is also very tasty. *Cost: 56¢ a container*, available in health food stores and some supermarkets.

Formulas require a lot of hygenic care since they're a garden for bacteria growth. The utensils for preparing the milk should be boiled, and the bottles sterilized. If you buy the concentrated liquids, boil tap water for 20 minutes and then cool it before you add it to the mixture. If you used bottled water, be sure it doesn't contain mineral salts. It's important to follow the directions accurately on the formula package to guarantee the right balance of ingredients.

Choosing a Formula   There are three types of formulas—concentrated liquids to which you add water, powdered mixes, and ready-to-feed cans. The latter are the most expensive and most convenient. Powdered mixes are, by far, the lowest priced. Three popular brands in all categories are SMA, Similac, and Enfamil. Different parents have different preferences, but it's all a question of what the ultimate consumer, your baby, has to say about it. All these formulas are well-balanced, but each baby's constitution is different, so your choice of formula may require some experimenting.

Manufacturers of infant formulas take extra precautions with their product. The vitamins and minerals that go into each batch of milk are premixed by another company and then sent to the manufacturers who mix the formulas. In 1985, there was an infant-formula recall because faulty premixes that had the wrong level of ingredients or were prepared in unsanitary conditions were discovered during FDA quarterly testings. The guilty company has since gone out of business, and manufacturers now test each batch of premix themselves. It has always been customary for Ross Laboratories, who produce Similac and Isomil (a soy-based formula), to test all the premixes they receive.

Whichever formula you choose, you can rely on it for total nutrition until your baby is 6 months old. In fact, experts say that breast or bottle should be the only food for an infant until about that time.

This may seem negligent to many grandmothers who were told to feed their children solids at the tender age of six weeks. They thought it would hasten a baby's achievement of that major developmental milestone—sleeping through the night. Now, physicians say, all it will hasten is allergies and indigestion. The baby's body in defense will produce antibodies. The early tongue-thrusting reflex is a natural protection against indigestible foods.

Starting Solid Foods Before your baby can eat solid food, his or her nervous system needs to mature enough to coordinate the tongue and jaw to swallow food placed in the mouth. At 4 to 6 months, a baby can use his or her tongue to move food to the back of the mouth and swallow. This is the age to feed your baby pureed fruits, vegetables, and cereals. At 8 to 12 months, a baby can move his or her jaw up and down and also has some lip control. Although a baby isn't ready for an adult meal, small amounts of solid food can be handled. Closer to one year, a baby can rotate food in the mouth and, with the help of some teeth, chew pretty well.

Baby Foods The baby food industry has always made it convenient to fatten up those little bodies. Before 1970 however, they weren't too careful about what went into the mouths of babes. Baby food in jars contained salt, MSG, artificial colorings, flavorings, and sugar. Thanks to the FDA and the consciousness of consumers, today's baby foods offer varying degrees of nutrition and good taste.

Earth's Best

Earth's Best is a new line of baby food produced in the Green Mountains from 100% organically grown produce. That means no pesticides or herbicides were used during the growing process; only botanical methods were used to control insects. All Earth's Best's foods are bought from certified organic growers and then lab-tested at the Earth's Best plant for any chemical residues. They use only whole foods, which means that their apple juice is pressed from whole apples, not from concentrate. Nothing is added except vitamin C, which is a heat-sensitive vitamin depleted by cooking. They have special cooking methods to minimize the sterilization time, thus producing a less compromised food. Earth's Best can exert high quality control since they produce all their foods at their own plant.

Earth's Best is the most delicious baby food we have tasted and the richest in color. *Cost: 89¢ a jar*, available in health food stores and some supermarkets.

Beech-Nut

Beech-Nut, Gerber, and Heinz have been called the "Big Three" of the baby food industry, and have all-improved the wholesomeness and variety of their products. Beech-Nut has come out with a four-phase feeding system call *Stages*. Foods are color-coded and labelled for different ages ranging from six months to toddlers. None contain artificial colors, flavors, modified starch, or MSG. Beech-Nut also puts complete nutritional labels on their meat products, which they're not required to do by law. *Cost: The price ranges from 3 for 89¢ to 59¢ a jar*, available in most supermarkets.

Note: As we go to press, Beech-Nut has been fined in Federal Court for selling artificially flavored apple drink labeled as apple juice. Beech-Nut no longer does business with the supplier of the offending concentrate and has adopted new testing procedures to insure against recurrence. The incident underlines the need for all parents to continually monitor quality control in an effort to give their baby only the best.

A Well-rounded Infant Diet

The Food and Nutrition Board of the National Academy of Sciences–National Research Council developed and regularly revises the recommended daily dietary allowances for infants. This list of proteins, vitamins, and minerals is the guideline for formula manufacturers. Babies under 1 year get most of their nutrition from milk or formula; solid foods, introduced after 6 months, are only supplements and gradually become a major nutritional source.

Babies' responses to solid foods are as diverse as their responses to people. Some will try to yank the spoon from your hand. Others will greet you, tight-lipped, and hurl the food across the kitchen. The baby who loves to eat gives her parents peace of mind. Although even the fussiest child won't starve herself, it's very upsetting to parents when a child refuses to eat.

We outline a basic diet with caution. It's common for babies to boycott everything but peaches and peas and still grow into healthy children. Offer your little one something from each basic food group but allow for flat refusals. Introduce each new food one at a time. Wait about a week before promoting another new food so you can easily identify which food may be causing indigestion or allergic reactions.

What Comes First

Most sources recommend introducing baby cereals and juices first, at 4 to 6 months. Cereals should be mixed with breast milk or formula. Even if your baby has a voracious appetite, start with only a few teaspoons a day. After a totally liquid diet, even a few spoonfuls of cereal can be constipating.

At 5 to 6 months, you can graduate to strained or mashed fruits, like banana and avacado, but avoid citrus. By 7 to 8 months, you may be up to two hearty meals a day or three smaller ones of fruit, cereal, and pureed vegetables. At about 9 months, add a little yogurt. During the latter part of the first year, you can offer meats, beans, breads, cottage cheese, and egg yolks. Consult your pediatrician about your individual baby's dietary needs and preferences.

How Much Is Enough?

The average 6 month old needs about 800 calories a day. If she drinks 32 ounces of formula or breast milk, she's already consumed 640 calories. By her first birthday, she may be drinking much less than that and have switched to about 16 ounces of cow's milk, which provides 288 calories. *Note:* Many babies show lactose intolerance and may have trouble digesting the proteins and sugars in cow's milk. Some seem to grow out of this intolerance in their second year.

The rest of a 1 year old's fuel should take the following distribution: four servings from the fruit and vegetable group, two from proteins such as meat, fish, eggs, tofu, or beans, and four servings of grains, like pasta, cereals, breads, and rice. The three suggested dairy servings are met by breast milk or cow's milk. A toddler serving may be quite small from the adult perspective, but a plate piled high with food may be overwhelming to a baby. Offer her a little at a time and always ask her if she'd like more.

Don't expect your baby to take your ideas about proper feeding from the four basic food groups very seriously. Over the first few years of eating solids, she may get a balanced diet, but it will require a broad perspective on your part. One healthy 4 year old ate dairy products the first year, fruit and vegetables the second, grains the third, and proteins the fourth. Parenting is a continual balancing act.

For additional reading try: *Into the Mouths of Babes; A Natural Foods Cookbook for Infants and Toddlers* by Susan Tate Firkaly, Better Way Publications, 1984, $6.95.

Let's Have Healthy Children by Adelle Davis, New American Library, $4.50.

Dr. Eden's Healthy Kids: The Essential Diet, Exercise and Nutrition Program by Alvin N. Eden, M.D. with Andrea Boyar, Ph.D., R.D., New American Library, $8.95.

Foods for Healthy Kids by Dr. Lendon Smith, Berkley Books, $3.95.

Heinz

Heinz has a new line of dehydrated baby foods that keep longer than foods in jars. There are 2 to 4 servings per container; just add water to the desired consistency, and put the rest of the flakes back on the shelf for future use. The reconstituted food is easy to swallow, but boring in texture. A redeeming factor is the absence of additives or modified starches. The problem with modified starches is that young infants may not fully digest them and undigested starches can cause diarrhea, which in turn, prevents babies from absorbing nutrients. The regular Heinz baby food in jars, as well as the Gerber products, may contain these ingredients; always check the labels. If nothing else, these starches give you less for your money. When Beech-Nut stopped adding starch and sugar to its strained bananas, it had to add twice the bananas! *Cost: 59¢ a container*, available in most supermarkets.

Best Feeding Gear

Best Feeding Gear

Whether you're breastfeeding or not, you'll still need a selection of bottles for water and juice. They fall into two categories: disposable bottles which are called nursers and permanent glass or plastic ones. Traditionally both types come in 4 ounce and 8 ounce sizes. Some parents prefer the disposables because they are presterilized. The bag collapses as a baby drinks and cuts down on air intake. They once saved on all that time spent on laborious sterilization, but today many pediatricians feel that sterilizing is no longer necessary and that the dishwasher does the trick.

Nipples usually come with bottles, generally in standard sizes; different types can be purchased separately. (One exception to this pattern is Playskool's Nŭrsa and Pŭr lines.) Be sure not to purchase too many nipples ahead of time. Babies develop preferences. Nipples are also sized according to age and food intake. Sizes roughly correspond to newborn, infant, and toddler. Besides four to five bottles if you are nursing and about twice that if you are bottle-feeding, you will need a good bottle brush. Insulated bags or containers designed to fit a bottle are also useful for when you and your baby are out and about more. If your pediatrician does recommend sterilizing bottles separately, you will also need a sterilizing unit. Most bottle lines have them and they can be purchased at the same time as everything else.

Because you are feeding both the child and the floor, raising this child will be expensive.

Bill Cosby

Best for Baby

Änsa

This company introduced the easy-to-hold bottle with a hole for small hands to grasp. It is one of the most popular bottle lines in America today. Many parents testify that their children really do prefer them.

The **Änsa** line is available in hard clear or pastel plastic. They recently added a nurser to their line with an indent instead of the doughnut, and it will accept any sterilized bags on the market. All bottles come in 4- and 9-ounce sizes, with both ounce and cubic centimeter markings. They include a cap and snap-on hood for travel. Nipples are either latex or silicone.

The **Änsa** line has the Good Housekeeping seal of approval. *Approximate retail: 4 oz. clear or plastic/$1.70–$1.80; 9 oz. clear or plastic/ $2.25–$2.50; nurser/$2.25–$3.00. Note:* Änsa also has printed bottles that cost a few nickels more.

Nuk by Gerber

This line of nipples and pacifiers is popular both here and in Europe. The nipples have a special orthodontic shape that is supposed to re-create the shape of a mother's nipple in the baby's mouth. The Nuk was invented by a doctor in Germany in 1950 and has had many rivals but no equals. It remains the orthodontic nipple of choice today.

The **Nuk** comes in three sizes of latex and will fit any standard 40-millimeter bottle opening. Gerber has three sizes of pacifier, also in latex, and a new nurser line. They have a full range of standard glass or plastic bottles to choose from, including a small medicine size. **Nuk** recently introduced a three-piece toothbrush training set. It includes two different soft gum massagers for teething infants and a soft toddler toothbrush for cleaning young teeth. *Approximate retail: Nuk standard nipples, 2/$2.50; Nuk pacifier/$1.60 each; Medi-Nurser sets/$2.75; Toothbrush training set/$6.39.*

Playskool Nŭrsa

This line popularized disposable bottles. Rather than bottles, per se, the **Nursa** line comes with holders. Into these fit presterilized nipple, bag, and cap sets. Fill the bag with formula, screw on the nipple/cap, and the bottle is ready to be used. The holders are punctuated by openings so you may monitor your baby's progress. The bag collapses as your baby feeds, allowing less air to be swallowed. Nipples are latex and sets are available in 4- and 8-ounce sizes. *Note:* Nŭrsa fits only its own nipple sets. *Approximate retail: Trial pack/$1.50; Overnight (8 feedings)/$3.50; Everyday pack (16 feedings)/$7.00; Individual cap sets: 12 pack/$5.00; 36 pack/$15.*

Playskool Pūr

This line of bottles and nipples is made from 100% medical-grade silicone. Silicone, unlike latex rubber, takes on no taste or odors. The nipples also hold their shape remarkably well; latex tends to droop and crack. (This tendency is not an inherent quality of rubber; the latex is broken down by enzymes in infant saliva.) Bottles come in 4- and 8-ounce sizes. Nipples come in regular or orthodontic styles in three sizes. The **Pūr** line also contains one-piece pacifiers in the three sizes and two nipple configurations. These all-in-one pacifiers are favored because they present no parts to come loose and choke an infant. One especially convenient item they also manufacture is a "mininurser."

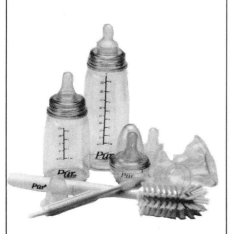

This small 1-ounce bottle fitted with its own nipple is perfect for delivering medicines to a sick baby. You grind up the aspirin or antibiotic and mix with juice. *Approximate retail: 4 oz. bottle, $1.90; 8 oz. bottle, $2.60; nipples, 2/$2.95; pacifier, $2.00; Medi-nurser, $3.00.*

Remond

Remond is a fabulous line of bottles and 100% natural rubber nipples from France imported by the Handy Chair Corporation. Because of their advantages, they are frequently used by French maternity hospitals and preemie units. Their special nipple air regulators sustain an inner pressure equal to the outside atmosphere. The nipple will therefore not collapse, nor can a baby suck the bottle empty. The regulators also prevent a child from eating too quickly, which is one of the main reasons for vomiting.

Remond bottles come in clearly marked 4- and 8-ounce sizes, in glass or polycarbonate. Their newborn nipple comes with holes pierced aslant so milk won't squirt directly into baby's throat. The

Pap Nipple has been designed for thicker food. A Vari-Nipple comes with three graduated positions, each opening an additional slit, which can be adjusted according to an infant's age, formula, or appetite. They have a thermal bottle available and a thermal bottle holder. Each bottle also comes with its own brightly colored cap for travel. *Note*: **Remond** has a preemie nipple (see page 149) and a nipple for babies with a cleft palate. *Approximate retail: 9 oz. bottles/$3.25–$3.50; 4 oz. bottles/$2.75–$3.00 (glass or polycarbonate). Nipples/$.75–$2.00 each (for specialty nipples).*

Best for Baby

Mag Mag Training Cup System

This system is particularly good for mothers switching a child from breastfeeding. The system comes with two bottles that are fat and short—more like cups. One has handles and the other a plastic swinging grip. Either bottle can be fitted with one of three graduated drinking spouts. The first is a regular latex nipple. For toddlers you can introduce a soft plastic spout with a wider opening. Once your infant is comfortable with that, you can begin substituting a firm plastic straw. Finally the whole lid comes off and you have a two-handled cup.

Bottles are both 8-ounce and double-walled for hygiene. They are assembled easily and all parts are interchangeable on either cup. Best of all, the cup can be attached to **Mag Mag's** electric breast pump and used as the collector. *Approximate retail: Mag Mag System with two bottles and three spouts, $17; bottles and spouts available separately for between $2 and $5; Mag Mag Breast Pump/$50.*

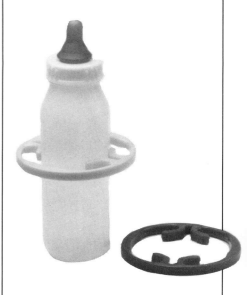

Ring Around

The **Ring Around** from A-Plus fits all standard bottles and is the answer to your baby's gripping problems if you don't use the Änsa. The ring is made from a durable nontoxic plastic and doubles as a teething bar. *A package of two—one red, one yellow—retails for $2.50.*

Deluxe High Chair by Gerry

One of the problems with high chairs is that parents often begin to use them too early when a baby still cannot properly support himself and eat at the same time. The Gerry seat you see here solves that problem nicely with its special curved back that hugs a child and provides more support. The seat also reclines and the footrest adjusts to accommodate growing children. The Gerry's large circular tray tilts away from your baby and can be removed with one hand. The entire seat pulls apart easily for cleaning nooks and crannies. Colors available are gray, periwinkle blue, or dusty rose. *Approximate retail: $69.*

Fisher-Price High Chair

There are plenty of fancier high chairs but few are as well-designed as this one. In fact, the company advertises that they consulted with over 2000 mothers before they perfected it. The seat is covered in a fabric-backed vinyl that wears better than regular vinyl. It also pops out for easy cleaning. The front tray—extra large to catch all that flying food and formula—slopes slightly down and away from your baby to let those spills collect. One hand also removes it easily, leaving the other free for an infant. The three-position footrest is suitable for all sizes of children. Best of all it folds flat for storage. Available in off-white with chrome legs and navy or tan seat. *Approximate retail: $73.*

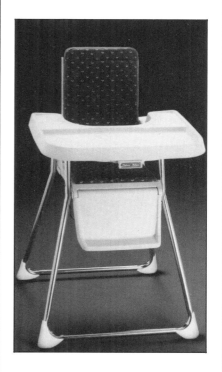

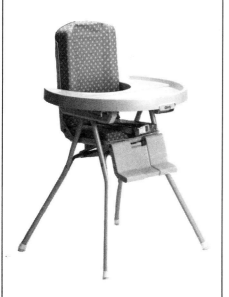

Best
Baby Books for Parents

Best Baby Books for Parents

The dawn of the modern era in parenting books broke in 1946 with the publication of *The Common Sense Book of Baby and Child Care* by a relatively unknown Manhattan pediatrician named Benjamin Spock. Until that time, the main authority in child raising was a turn-of-the-century doctor named Luther Emmet Holt. Holt's methods were so strict and his admonitions so peremptory that today he seems downright barbarous. He advocated potty training at *2 months* and discouraged rocking a child or comforting her in any way. It was "a habit easily acquired and hard to break." Never play with your baby before the age of 4 months, he continued, and then only in the morning.

Psychological Care of Infant and Child by John B. Watson, another popular reference from the same period, was not much gentler. Watson stated, "Never, never kiss your child." The U.S. Children's Bureau published a pamphlet on baby care that was only slightly more tolerant. Their recommendation: "If you must, kiss them once on the forehead when they say goodnight. Shake hands with them in the morning."

In this atmosphere Spock's book was a revelation. For the first time a respected professional acted as if children were full human beings. His emphasis on the emotional development and happiness of a child was embraced by postwar parents everywhere. Even today when Spock is considered passé by many, his book still sells a million copies a year worldwide. In truth, although there are many excellent alternatives, few new mothers have the confidence *not* to buy Spock even if they never do use it.

The fields of pediatrics, child psychology, and women's medicine have flourished in the past forty years. The long list of fine books available on all aspects of childbirth and child rearing reflect this growth. Happy reading!

The best way to give advice to your children is to find out what they want and advise them to do it.

Harry S. Truman

Every child is born a genius.

R. Buckminster Fuller

Best for Baby

Pregnancy and Childbirth

The Complete Book of Pregnancy and Childbirth by Sheila Kitzinger, Knopf, 1986, $17.95.

This is a thorough and wise look at pregnancy and childbirth that covers everything from conception to the baby's first ten days. It is well-illustrated and the quality of both the drawings and photos is excellent. The women and men in the illustrations are people from real life, not models, which reflects the author's humane and sympathetic attitude toward her readers.

Kitzinger is a childbirth educator, the author of seven previous books on childbirth and mothering, and the mother of five children. A social anthropologist and long-time champion of women's childbirth rights, she has studied methods of childbirth education all over the globe and has been developing her own approach since 1958. She lectures, teaches, and is on the Advisory Board of England's National Childbirth Trust.

A Child is Born (Revised Edition), with photographs by Lennart Nilsson, text by Mirjam Furuhjelm, Axel Ingelman-Sundberg, and Claes Wirsen, drawings by Bernt Forsblad. Dell/Seymour Lawrence, 1986, $12.95.

Lennart Nilsson is a pioneer in the field of scientific medical photography. His pictures of a baby, from the moment of conception through fetal development and birth, are awe-inspiring. The text is informative but the photographs are the real reason for buying this book.

○

What to Expect When You're Expecting and What to Eat When You're Expecting by Arlene Eisenberg, Heidi Eisenberg Merkoff, and Sandy Eisenberg Hathaway, R.N., Workman, $7.95 each.

These are simple, straightforward guides by the same mother-daughter team. The eating guide is organized around various stages of motherhood: while you're breastfeeding, between children, and of course during pregnancy itself. It includes over 100 recipes. The guide to expecting is broken down into months. The authors draw on their own experiences as mothers in addressing their audience. Both volumes are well-designed.

The Experience of Childbirth (Fifth Edition) by Sheila Kitzinger, Puffin, 1984, $5.95.

This book mainly explores the process of labor itself, but also goes into other issues like modern obstetrical practices, sex during pregnancy, and drugs in common use. Kitzinger concludes with a discussion of the emotional and psychological aspects of childbearing and the changes for both partners in the new role of parent. Another outstanding book.

o

Pregnancy, Childbirth and the Newborn by Penny Simkin, R.P.T., Janet Whalley, R.N., B.S.N., and Ann Keppler, R.N., M.N., Meadowbrook, 1984, $9.95.

This is another very thorough guide to birth experience from conception to feeding your new baby. The book is clear, well-illustrated, practical, and honest. The authors discuss the many choices to make about childbirth options and make a particular effort to describe labor as a normal physiological process instead of the illness it is commonly represented to be. They also go into the role of the father in the birth process in some detail.

All three women are professionals and childbirth educators. Their approach is reassuring and thorough.

Practical How-to Child-rearing Guides

Dr. Spock's Baby and Child Care by Benjamin Spock, M.D. and Michael Rothenberg, M.D., 1985 Edition, Pocket Books, $4.95.

Spock has come a long way from the time he used "him" to refer to the baby and "her" to refer to the mother. This latest edition also sports a younger co-author. But the numbered format retained from earlier editions strikes us as dated and simplistic. His psychological analyses still err on the side of too much Freud and not enough Jung. The book does have an outstanding index that's useful for child illnesses. Recommended for use in tandem with other guides and with our due respect.

o

First Year Baby Care by Paula Kelly, M.D., Meadowbrook, 1983, $5.95.

This is a thorough and compact guide that answers many of the questions new parents have on how to care for their child. The photos and drawings are clear and useful.

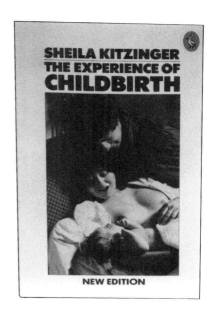

Best for Baby

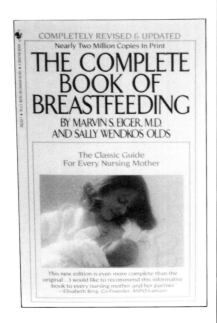

The First Six Months, Your Baby and Child, and *Your Growing Child* by Penelope Leach, Knopf, 1987, 1978, and 1983, $14.95 each.

For us, Leach has replaced Spock as the preeminent child-rearing expert to consult. All three of these works are general reference guides to all aspects of your child's growth and development during a specific period. *Your Growing Child* is the most comprehensive of the group, covering birth through adolescence. The encyclopedia format makes it a handy book to reach for when problems arise, and the advice she gives is balanced and well-researched. Leach covers difficult issues like death with remarkable sensitivity.

The First Six Months is not really a how-to with information on diapering or feeding. Rather it deals lovingly and gently with the emotional development of the first 6 months. Dr. Leach takes things from the baby's point of view and dispells such old wives' tales as "Babies cry to exercise their lungs." Lovely photographs by John Campbell.

Your Baby and Child concentrates on the period from birth to age 5. Library Journal said in its review that if you were to purchase one book of childcare advice, this should be it. It has over 650 illustrations plus numerous charming color photographs. Like Leach's other books, it is full of sound and sensible advice. It contains a thorough discussion of the various psychological changes and behavioral developments your child will go through. She says at one point that she had the good fortune to be part of a close, extended family; it's the good fortune of her readers as well. *Your Baby and Child* also has one of the best indexes we've ever seen.

Leach was educated at Cambridge University and took a Ph.D. from the London School of Economics in Social Psychology. She is married and the mother of two children. One of Britain's foremost childcare authorities, she ran a four-year national study on the effects of babies on their parents.

o

The Complete Book of Breastfeeding (Revised Edition) by Marvin Eiger, M.D. and Sally Wendkos Olds, Bantam, 1987, $5.95.

This is the classic text in the field. Comprehensive and indispensable. Highly recommended for any nursing mother.

Parenting Practices

On Becoming a Family, Infants and Mothers (Revised Edition), and *Working and Caring* by T. Berry Brazelton, M.D., Dell, Dell, and Addison-Wesley respectively, 1981, 1983, and 1987, $12.95, $13.95, and $18.95.

These are three excellent works by T. Berry Brazelton of Harvard Medical School and Chief of the Child Development Unit at Boston Children's Hospital. They are filled with solid advice and information about the parenting process starting with birth and continuing through to the return to work full-time by both parents. His work does contain a discernible male bias of the conventional sort, but the books are nonetheless sound.

P.E.T. Parent Effectiveness Training by Dr. Thomas Gordon, New American Library, 1970, $7.95.

Hundreds of thousands of parents have used the P.E.T. course as a way to bridge the gap between themselves and their children. The kids benefit and so do the parents. Typical results are: less fighting, warmer relationships, reasonable rules established, more responsible children, and genuine friendship between child and parent. Many people swear by these methods.

o

The Parent's Guide to Raising Twins by Elizabeth Freidrich and Cherry Rowland, St. Martin's Press, 1984, $15.95.

Freidrich and Rowland are both mothers of twins. Their book deals with the problems —and joys—of having more on your hands than you expected. They discuss everything from labor and breastfeeding for two, to what to do when you just can't cope. Extensive quotes from other parents of twins.

Best for Baby

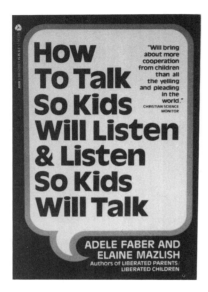

Child Psychology

Siblings without Rivalry by Adele Faber and Elaine Mazlish, Norton, 1987, $14.95.

Fighting, squabbling, and teasing produces a family stress that takes its toll on everyone. Authors Faber and Mazlish present effective ways to reduce the rivalry and promote cooperation. This book recently graced the New York Times bestseller list, which indicates just how widespread these problems are. Take heart. With help from the ideas and approaches outlined by various case studies, life in a family can be easier. Both authors are childcare educators and parents themselves.

o

How to Talk So Kids Will Listen and Listen So Kids Will Talk by Faber and Mazlish, Avon, 1980, $5.95.

Another no-nonsense discussion of a key aspect of successful childraising. Deservedly popular.

Your One Year Old, Your Two Year Old, etc. by Louise Bates Ames, Frances Ilg, and Carol Chase Haber, Dell, 1982, $7.95 each.

This is a series of four titles from the Gesell Institute of Child Development. Each one takes an in-depth look at one year's development and maturity. They are knowledgeable and informative, if somewhat academic in tone.

o

Your Child's Self-esteem by Dorothy Corkville Briggs, Doubleday Dolphin, 1975, $8.95.

Widely considered a classic on this important subject. Briggs's thesis is that all growth and behavior should be seen against the backdrop of the child's search for identity and self-respect. She feels that children value themselves to the extent they have been valued. What's more, becoming a parent does not confer any special knowledge about how to raise a confident child. This book is a solid instructional guide for parents to help children create strong feelings of self-worth. The author has been a teacher, psychologist, and family and child counselor for more than twenty-five years. Highly recommended.

Theoretical and Inspirational

Whole Child, Whole Parent by Polly Berrien Berends, Harper & Row, 1983, $10.95.

Berends's book, with a foreword by M. Scott Peck, is just what the title implies: a holistic look at the parenting process. She uses child raising as a means of inquiring what the essence of being human is about. A great deal of practical information as well.

o

A Good Enough Parent by Bruno Bettelheim, Knopf, 1987, $18.95.

Bettelheim asserts that there is no such thing as a perfect parent, and that rather we should aim to become a "good enough parent" in as creative a way as we can find. He strongly feels that raising a child is an art, not a science. The breadth and scope of the book as well as this man's humaneness are inspirational.

Dr. Bettelheim is the Distinguished Professor of Education and Professor of Psychiatry at the University of Chicago. He is the author of a number of books on children including *The Uses of Enchantment*, which won the National Book Award in 1977.

The Nurturing Father by Kyle Pruett, M.D., Warner, 1987, $18.95.

Fathers are taking a more active role in the parenting process. Pruett celebrates the success of the "nurturing father." He examines cases of couples who have reversed the standard gender roles, where the father is the prime caregiver. The results are heartening and inspiring. This book is a *must* for new fathers.

Pruett is Clinical Professor of psychiatry at Yale University Child Study Center.

o

Prisoners of Childhood/The Drama of the Gifted Child by Alice Miller, Basic Books, 1981, $7.95.

If you read one theoretical book about child rearing, let this be the one. Miller compassionately and passionately examines the plight of a gifted (read sensitive) child adjusting his or her own behavior to meet the emotional needs of the parent. The result is repression of the child's own true feelings and loss of the true self as an adult. There's not a person we know who won't see themselves in the emotional patterns described in this book. In other words, all children are gifted. Highly recommended.

Best Books for Ages 6 Months to 4 Years

Best Books for Ages 6 Months to 4 Years

Until 200 years ago, children began to read by learning their ABC's. They each had a hornbook, a small wooden board shaped like a ping-pong paddle, with the alphabet written out on a sheet of paper in the shape of a Latin cross. This paper was covered with a thin sheet of transparent horn, hence the name. Memorization of the letters usually began at the age of 3. Children were required to learn the alphabet backwards, forwards, and in any spontaneous order their teacher called out before they were considered really proficient. This process could last anywhere between one and five years. Meanwhile, they studied *nothing else.*

Once they had mastered the alphabet, they moved on to letter combinations or syllables. After every conceivable syllable had been pounded into their brains, assumption held that they would be able to read. Since in fact they could not read (the assumption was false), the by-now exhausted teacher began to teach the thoroughly dumbfounded students actual words. That reading was perceived by many children to be a thoroughly boring subject to be avoided at all costs is of little wonder.

Around the mid-eighteenth century various enterprising European scholars started children reading with whole books. They went a little overboard, however. One man is recorded as starting toddlers on a 400-page version of the adventures of Telemachus in quest of his father Ulysses, long overdue from the Trojan war.

When their American counterparts began to employ the new methods, they luckily choose easier material. By the early nineteenth century more and more children were learning to read by the so-called

"What is the use of a book," thought Alice, *"without pictures or conversation?"*

Lewis Carroll

The Caldecott Medal

This medal is awarded annually to the most distinguished American picture book for children. It is named after Randolph Caldecott, a famous English children's illustrator. The medal celebrates its fiftieth anniversary in 1988. The ten most recent winners are:

Hey, Al, Egielski and Yorinks (Farrar)

The Polar Express, Van Allsburg (Houghton Mifflin)

Saint George and the Dragon, Hyman (Little, Brown)

The Glorious Flight, Provensens (Viking)

Shadow, Brown (Scribner)

Jumanji, Van Allsburg (Houghton Mifflin)

Fables, Lobep (Harper)

Ox-Cart Man, Cooney (Viking)

The Girl Who Loved Wild Horses, Goble (Bradbury)

Noah's Ark, Spier (Doubleday)

whole word method. One enlightened educator began small children with a few simple words, following with the alphabet which they then easily apprehended, followed by more difficult words and sentence structures.

This new method was not universally met with approval. One prominent professor decried the new word method as reducing English "to the status of Chinese," depriving children of the benefits of a language based on *letters*. He buttressed this argument by adding that it was wrong to make anything pleasant or easy for a young student. This struggle lasted most of the century.

By early in this century, the word method of teaching to read was widely accepted. But thirty years later, an interesting phenomenon was observed. Adults who once read very well seemed to lose most of their ability if for some reason their reading was interrupted for an extended period. Educators began to realize that things had gone too far in the opposite direction. If people really did learn only whole words, they had no skills by which to figure out the pronunciation of a new (or old) word. Phonics was reintroduced to the study of reading. Today, most reading programs have evolved to include wide applications of both methods.

One way to turn your child into a reader is to start early. Children's books have blossomed in the past 100 years. There are heaps of wonderful books to choose from for the youngest possible readers on up. Below is a list of twenty-one titles for children under age 4 that they will enjoy long after that age. They are broken into three categories: wordless books, pattern books, and story books, plus one Mother Goose.

Wordless Books

These books are appropriate for the newest readers. They're great because a parent can spend as much or as little time on each page as the child desires. Since there are no words, they also coax both child and parent to really *look*.

A Story To Tell by Dick Bruna, Price-Stern, $2.95.

Bruna is a well-known Dutch illustrator. His book is the story of encountering everyday objects. Lovely, simple graphics.

The Baby's Catalogue by Allan and Janet Ahlberg. Little, Brown, hardcover, $14.95, paperback, $5.95

This is a large, colorful book with lots of things about babies. There's a whole page on diapers, for example. The book is multicultural and depicts babies engaged in all sorts of activities. Infants we know just love to look at this book because it, well, has to do with what they're most interested in.

How Do I Put It On? by Watanabe Shigeo, Putnam, hardcover, $8.95.

This is a book full of inverted, silly jokes about putting on and wearing clothes by a terrific Japanese illustrator.

Freight Train by Donald Crews, Greenwillow Books, hardcover, $11.75, Puffin paperback, $3.95

This is a marvelous graphic concept book. It leads the eye from left to right following from the engine right through to the caboose until all that's left is a puff of smoke and the tracks.

Sunshine by Jan Omerod, Lothrop, hardcover, $10.25, Puffin paperback, $2.95

This book follows a day in the life of children. The youngsters are done in a way that renders them genderless. The dad has a beard and cooks.

Caps For Sale by Esphyr Slobodkina, Harper & Row, hardcover, $8.95, paperback, $2.95

A cap peddler falls asleep under the tree and the monkeys steal his caps. He screams, shakes his fist, and stamps his feet, but all the monkeys do is mimick his actions. It is not until he throws his own cap down on the ground in disgust that they do the same, and he gets all the caps back. Kids love to laugh at an adult throwing a tantrum. It helps give them a perspective on their own anger too.

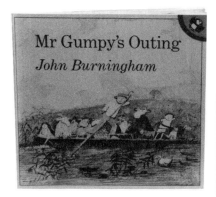

Pattern Books

Pattern books are often in rhyme. They are for the slightly older child who likes to experiment and play with words. These children often needs things repeated at this stage as well. Pattern books help to do this both visually and linguistically.

Johnny Crow's Garden by Leslie Brooke, Warner, paperback, $4.95

This turn-of-the-century British book has recently been reissued. The book is in verse and all about animals. Full of nonsense that children love.

Goodnight Moon by Margaret W. Brown, Harper & Row, hardcover, $8.95, paperback, $2.95

This is the one book that virtually all children love. A rhyming story in which a bunny first names all the objects in the room and then says goodnight to each, one by one, as the pages grow progressively darker.

Mr. Gumpy's Outing by John Burningham, Holt, Rinehart and Winston, hardcover, $10.95, Puffin paperback, $3.50

This is the story of Mr. Gumpy crossing the river. The deal is he allows all the neighboring children and animals along as long as they behave. Of course they don't and their mischief sets up a chain reaction whereupon they all end up in the water. This is a cumulative pattern book: it builds to a climax that results in a satisfying ending.

Where the Wild Things Are by Maurice Sendak, Harper & Row, hardcover, $11.95, paperback, $4.95

This is a fanciful story by the reigning genius of picture books. Four-year-old Max has a fight with his mother and leaves to go "where the wild things are." Max, at first scared, tames the beasts by staring them down. It ends with a happy resolution of Max's problems with his mother.

Mother Goose Illustrated by Brian Wildsmith, Oxford University Press, hardcover, $12.95, paperback, $7.95

The age-old rhymes for children, one per page, amidst very colorful drawings.

Story Books

Millions of Cats by Wanda Gag, Coward/McCann, hardcover, $6.95, paperback, $2.95

This is the tale of a lonely old couple who long for a cat to keep them company. The husband sets off, finds a field with millions of cats, and decides to pick the prettiest one. Of course each time he lifts his head, he spies another even prettier cat. In no time he has chosen them all. When he arrives home, his wife says they really must choose only one. With this the millions of cats begin to fight. When the couple next looks outside, all the cats are gone except one thin, frightened scraggly kitten, which they keep.

The Snowy Day by Ezra J. Keats, Viking, hardcover, $11.95, Puffin paperback, $3.95

This is a lovely quiet story of one little boy's exploration of a city snowfall. He tries to take it all home by putting a snowball in his pocket, but it melts by the time he goes to bed. That night he dreams that all the snow has melted but awakens to find that there is even more than yesterday. It has snowed all night and he sets off to find a friend to help him play.

Blueberries for Sal by Robert McCloskey, Viking, hardcover, $11.95, Puffin paperback, $3.50

A mother and her daughter and a mother bear and her female cub each go berry picking to store up food for winter. Both Sal and the cub wander from their mothers and end up innocently behind the wrong mother. The mothers go in search of their own offspring, identifying their daughters by the different sounds they make picking the berries. They calmly proceed down opposite sides of the mountain, picking and eating as they go.

The Tale of Peter Rabbit by Beatrix Potter. Warner, hardcover, $4.95, paperback, $2.95

The famous tale of Peter the young rabbit who disobeys his mother's express orders and heads straight to Mr. MacGregor's vegetable patch. The tale is primarily about Peter's comical and near calamitous escape. That night, feeling unwell, he gets nothing but chamomile tea for dinner, while his better behaved siblings get blackberries, milk, and bread.

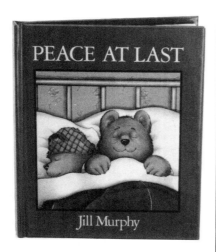

The Very Hungry Catepillar by Eric Carle, Putnam, hardcover, $12.95, in miniature, $3.95

A subtle but very colorful concept book. The story begins with a catepillar that hatches from an egg on a leaf. The catepillar is very hungry and eats his way through the week, increasing the numbers of objects he eats every day. Finally he forms a cocoon and emerges as a beautiful butterfly.

Play With Me by Marie H. Ets, Viking, hardcover, $13.95, Puffin paperback, $3.95

This book is illustrated in gentle pastels. It shows a young child, the reader's peer, chasing one animal after another until they finally learn how to make friends—by not chasing.

Ask Mr. Bear by Marjorie Flack, Macmillan, hardcover, $10.95, paperback, $3.95

This is the story of a little bear trying to find the perfect present for mother. In the end, they discover together that the perfect gift is a hug. A great book to cuddle up with.

Where's Spot? by Eric Hill, Putnam, hardcover, $10.95

This is a story about a playful puppy hiding from mom. She goes looking in a variety of places. Here the child lifts up flaps in the book finding that, no, the puppy is not there. Of course in the end the puppy is found. Children relish the anticipation even though they quickly memorize the answers.

Peace At Last by Jill Murphy, Dial, hardcover, $11.50, paperback, $3.50

This is another cumulative story. Father bear has trouble getting to sleep because of all the night sounds.

Books for Parents

The Read-Aloud Handbook by Jim Trelease, Penguin, paperback, $6.95.

Trelease's thesis is basically that reading aloud to children encourages them to read themselves. He feels that the time spent reading aloud is as precious as any particular book in laying the foundations of the reading habit. His section on the effects of TV may move you to banish it for good.

Babies Need Books by Marie Butler, Atheneum (out of print).

As we go to press, this oustanding and important work is unavailable from the publisher. If it does not go back to print, we strongly suggest trying to find it at the library. Butler explores reading for infants through 6 year olds and concludes each chapter with an excellent reading list. Many educators and reading specialists feel that it's the best book ever written on the subject.

Horn Book, Inc.

This name, evocative of misery for so many generations, now denotes a great organization devoted to furthering the interests of top-quality children's books. For $3 you can send for "Children's Classics: A Book List for Parents." For $30 per year, you can subscribe to the Horn Book Magazine, which reviews the best new children's books and is the bible of many librarians in the field. Contact:

Horn Book, Inc.
31 St. James Avenue
Boston, MA 02116
(617) 482-5198

International Reading Association

This organization puts out eight different booklets on various aspects of helping your child to read. They are well-written and accessible. Send an envelope with postage for 4 ounces to receive all eight. Write to:

International Reading
  Association
800 Barksdale Road
Newark, DE 19714

Best Daycare
and How to Judge It

Best Daycare

We think of day care as a modern phenomenon, but actually its ancestral line goes back to the mid-nineteenth century. Although most working parents relied on neighbors and extended families, in the worst of times, children wandered the streets. (Many safety-conscious parents tied their children to a bedpost until they returned home!) Finally the roaming young populace grew so numerous that horrified society ladies pooled their resources and started day nurseries to accomodate these "wastrels." A few of these nurseries were even sponsored by employers. Local regulatory boards developed and almost immediately restricted nursery hours for infants. Instead, these boards emphasized care for the close-to-kindergarten set, and day nurseries gave way to nursery schools. Working moms in need of infant care were on their own again until World War II sent the working dads overseas. Federal and local governments, suddenly dependent on women for a domestic workforce, sponsored the return of day nurseries.

The men returned home and day nurseries vanished as quickly as they'd come. We entered the postwar era to the tune of "Leave It to Beaver" and "Donna Reed." Moms stayed at home, and by the 1950s nursery schools had become a social frill for the middle class. It wasn't until the sixties' war on poverty, fight for equality, and rise of feminism that childcare again became an issue, especially for the poor. By the seventies, the concept of IQ modifiability, demonstrated in head start programs for poverty-level children, was extended to all preschoolers. Excitement rose in the professional community and spilled over to parents. Recession and inflation brought day cares back again, with a new twist: early education could make our kids smarter and better—a first step in getting ahead.

The hardest job kids face today is learning good manners without seeing any.

Fred Astaire

The thing that impresses me most about America is the way parents obey their own children.

Duke of Windsor

Deductions for Childcare under the Current Tax Law

The deduction for care of a child under age 5 is 30% of employment expenses (for example, day care, house-keeper for child, cook for child) for a taxpayer with an adjusted gross income of $10,000 or less. This percentage decreases by 1% for each $2000 of additional income but cannot fall below 20%. In other words, for adjusted incomes above $28,000, the credit is 20% of day-care costs.

This credit can be claimed by (*a*) a married couple filing a joint return and both employed unless one is a student or disabled, (*b*) married individuals living apart: *one* can claim the credit on a separate return if she/he has a separate household for which she/he furnishes over half the cost during a taxable year, and from which the other spouse is absent at least 6 months of the year, (*c*) divorced parents and stepchildren for the parent having custody for the longer period.

From 1973 to 1983, the income for young families dropped over 16%. Moms joined the rush hour traffic, and the need for childcare, once a problem of women and the poor, became a priority of men and the middle class. Formerly, men were insulated from the stresses of who's minding the kids. Now both men and women wear the problem on their blue, white, or corporate sleeve. This time around, however, we're not just looking for babysitters. Accompanying us into the 1990s is a heated controversy about what constitutes quality care, where to find it, and who's going to foot the bill.

The decision to enroll a young child in day care is often fraught with guilt. There are so many potholes in the road to adjusted adulthood that it's pretty difficult for even the most conscientious, well-designed study of human development to isolate the ones that may give us our emotional flat tires. Some say what's most like mom is best: children need that one-on-one, intimate interaction complete with the mundane, daily experiences of grocery shopping, car repairs, and bank deposits. Recent research main-

tains that babies who receive more than 20 hours a week of nonparental care run the risk of psychological harm, manifested by insecure relationships and increased aggression.

Proponents of day care accuse those on the other side of the fence of chauvinism. They say that happy parents make happy kids, and a mother at home who wishes to work, or a family in financial distress, runs as much risk of producing maladjusted children as their stay-at-work counterparts. Their research on children in day care shows that these kids are more advanced socially, linguistically, and intellectually. Another argument in favor of group care is the magnet theory: kids are naturally drawn to other kids and thrive on this type of setting.

The day-care dilemma doesn't end with "to be or not to be." If you decide in favor of group care, there's the question of setting (whether you want home- or center-based child care) not to mention that of childrearing philosophy.

Center-based Care:

Day-care centers come in many shapes and sizes: private, university-affiliated, lab schools, church-affiliated, and employee-sponsored. Some are non-profit, others are franchised. There are special day cares for kids with a fever and others that hand you your offspring at 6:00 p.m. with a fresh haircut and dinner-to-go. The hours may be full-time or part-time; the policy may be structured, open, child-centered, teacher-centered, mixed age groups, single age groupings. Any one of these situations can be wonderful or disastrous. Quality of care is the crucial issue. To illustrate what makes a good center, we've highlighted a few exemplary day cares and their advice for judging centers in your area. Although the programs differ, each will give you an idea of what to aim for.

Day-Care Referrals

California Child Care Resource and Referral Center Network
809 Lincoln Way
San Francisco, CA 94122
(415) 661-1714

This organization publishes a national information and referral directory that can be had for $20.

Child Care Information Service
National Association for the
  Education of Young Children
1834 Connecticut Avenue NW
Washington, D.C. 20009

This organization will put you in touch with your city's or state's referral and resource agency. They also provide educational videos and brochures on areas of parenting and child development.

Bank Street Family Center, New York City. The Bank Street Center is affiliated with the Bank Street College of Education, reknowned for its work in early childhood development. It's a day-care facility for children 6 months to 3 years old. Its philosophy is that a good center should imitate a good home, not a school. The groups are small, nine or ten children in each, with three or more adults per group. The 10 to 30 month olds are together, with not more than two children under 12 months in one group. This mixed age grouping requires more adult supervision, but the Bank Street staff feel that it pays off in richer interactions. It is also more interesting for caregivers. Children aged 2 ½ to 3 form another group.

The center has an open-door parent policy, meaning parents are welcome to drop in anytime. In fact, only families who live or work in the Bank Street area can enroll in the program, insuring parent involvement. They have a slow and careful entry process; children start with a short day and gradually work up to their allotted hours. This process is individualized for each family so there are "no crying parents and no crying children."

Advice. Nancy Balaban of Bank Street's Work and Family Life Center says first look for an open-door policy. Be sure you're welcome. Visit awhile and see if the center's beliefs about children are compatible with yours. Think about what you'd do with your child if she or he were home with you and look for a center that approximates that. She tells staff at Bank Street, "If you need to go to the bank, take some kids with you. That's what they'd do at home." Too often programs use the nursery school model for children under 3, and it just doesn't fit. Kids that age need their own tempo.

Look for an environment that's clean and cheerful, with materials that invite kids to manipulate them, not gimmicky toys. There should be lots of gross motor activity—rolling and jumping, not sitting down. As for infants, they need to be held, carried, and talked to. Be discriminating when there's talk of stimulation; that can be overdone. Babies need to be smiled and cooed at more than they need to be read to.

Harvard Medical Area Children's Center, Boston. This center is housed in a building that belongs to Harvard Medical School. Harvard provides the space, maintainence, and materials free of charge. In return, Harvard-affiliated families get first dibs, which means about 75–80% of the enrollment. The other slots are available to the general public. Infants (3–15 months) have a special sleep room, a separate playroom, and a private cranny with a large mirror for intimate interludes with their reflections. Toddlers (15–33 months) have a separate space. Each playroom has a book corner, a place for art or messy materials, and a climbing loft with play area underneath. The climbing lofts have carpeted ramps; the infant ramp is equipped with dowels under the padding for small toes to grip. Opportunities are set up for the important business of dress-up, housekeeping, and play with manipulative toys, like blocks and puzzles. Materials are varied on a weekly basis; the approach is child-initiated. Basically, this means the kids decide what they'll do. Caregivers are down on the floor to help little ones get engaged in play. There's no formal circle time announcing daily plans. Children explore at their own level.

Best for Baby

The staff here also try to meet parents at their level. They have a primary caregiver system, which means that you get a morning and an afternoon personal liason. A morning and afternoon staff person is assigned to your family, and they keep daily charts of your child's participation, pleasures, and peeves. It's a kind of third link in the bonding process, keeping parents, children, and staff in communication. (Bank Street prefers to let these attachments develop spontaneously.)

Advice. Nancy Lauter-Clatell, of Boston's Wheelock College, which specializes in early childhood development, cited the Harvard Medical Area Center as exemplary. Her preference is for small centers that clearly regard families as part of the program and are small enough to individually address their needs. She, too, believes that most models for early care come from preschools and are then watered down for toddlers. The structure is too rigid; at 14–30 months, kids are busy all the time. Setting up times for specific things to happen is inappropriate.

She advises that when you're observing prospective centers, go in with an infant or toddler's eyes. Materials should be from floor level to 30 inches high. Look for versatile materials, like a set of colored plastic bowls that a baby can bang on, roll, stack, and wear; water, sand, mattresses to jump on, toys to share, not fight over. Children in this age group need sensory experiences and that means body in, not just hands on. Caregivers must have a sense of playfulness, for play is the work of children and is the source of linguistic and intellectual development.

Glendale Child Development Center, Minneapolis.
The Glendale Center is situated in the middle of a
housing project, yet 70% of their enrollment are the
children of yuppies. This is an environmentally based
program, so the first criterion is that it be a nice place
to spend the day, which translates into a nice place to
spend a childhood. Outside there's a playground built
by low-income teenagers. It's designed to be a small-
scale replica of the world, with experiences for every
sense and every muscle. This infant/toddler park has a
built-in stream, smells of all varieties, rough and
smooth objects, all landscaped into a child's wonder-
land. Inside there are lofts, platforms, plants, and
birds. It's a homelike center with challenges for young
learners built directly into the surroundings.

They, too, have a primary caregiver system,
which means that every child has a particular staff
member keeping track of his or her activities. They've
also devised administrative systems, like question-
naires and "congratulations on your first day of sepa-
ration" notes, to foster the parent connection.

Advice. Jim Greenman, who helped set up the Glendale Center, says that when you enroll your child in a
program you're buying that organization, so look carefully at the administration. Each center will have their
own "program culture." Once you get a sense of this,
find out how you fit in. You should feel that you have
as much control as you would with someone in your
own home.

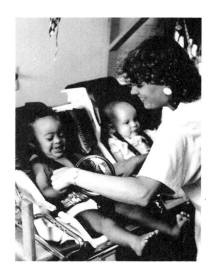

The Childcare Questions

Beside the simple questions, "Am I being a good parent?" or "What effect will this have on my baby in 20 years?," here are three categories of queries to help you organize your approach and choices.

Environment

• *Do I want my baby close to my home or my work place?* Close to work may allow for more midday visits, but can also mean a harried commute for both of you.

• *Is the center clean, cheerful, and free of toxic substances?*

• *Are babies separated from the potentially harmful toys of older children?*

• *How is the traffic flow? Is there easy access to materials and different areas of the room?*

• *For infants, is the room overly custodial with schedules for feeding and changing? Is the area homey?* While toddler programs are often watered-down preschools, infant programs take their cues from hospitals, the only model of group care for babies.

• *Is there comfortable seating to feed babies?*

Administration

• *Is there an open-door policy for parents?*

• *What systems are in place for good parent-center communication?*

• *What's the staff:child ratio?* Look for at least 1:3 for infants and 1:5 for toddlers.

• *How is the center funded?*

• *Who established the center?* University-affiliated programs, unlike lab schools, may not be associated with faculty at all. Find out the qualifications of the people who conceptualized the program. Consulting firms are sprouting up to help businesses establish day-care centers. Although some of these are staffed by educators, others are business-oriented. They know a lot about profit but not about people.

• *Who makes decisions? A board of directors? Staff? Parents?*

• *What's the staff turnover?* The average in this country is a disheartening 40% per year.

• *Does the program tend to stay close to full enrollment?* Be wary of long established programs that are underenrolled. This may be a sign of internal troubles or previous complaints.

Philosophy
• *What's the overall tone? Warm, flexible, supportive?*

• *What's the procedure for the day? Is it structured with a lot of sit-down time, or is it more child-centered?*

• *How does the program fit with your child's developmental stage, style, and interests?*

• *Are the materials multipurpose and creative? Do they nurture curiosity?*

• *How often do the children go outside?*

• *Do the caregivers seem affectionate and sincere with children and attentive to you?*

• *Would you want to spend the day there?*

Referrals

When looking for names of potential second homes for your infant or toddler, try some of the following sources. Resource and referral agencies; municipal agencies that regulate day cares; principals of schools near your home or work; religious institutions; universities with early childhood programs; reputable nursery schools; friends; your pediatrician; your prenatal instructor or advertisements. Start looking early; there are centers around the country with files labelled "Preconception." Good centers, especially those that take infants, may have two-year waiting lists. *Cost: $35–$200 a week.*

For additional referral information see addresses at end of section.

Home-based or Family Day Care

Many families prefer this kind of care, especially for very young children. As always, there are pros and cons.

Pros: The setting is homelike. Children take naps on beds, instead of mats on the floor, and lunch is at the kitchen table. The age grouping is usually mixed, simulating a real family. If the caregiver is doing this work for a supplemental income and a love of kids, you often get momlike care. The hours are more flexible than day-care centers and may accommodate part-time hours and erratic schedules. If you find a great caregiver, your child can stay with her for years, offering another secure adult relationship in a child's hectic life.

Cons: One person at home alone with a bunch of kids may go crazy. There's something sane about having other adults with you. These caregivers may have little or no training in child development and may have 18 month olds lined up in front of the couch at 9 a.m. every morning, reciting the "Pledge of Allegiance." (A true case story). Toys may be scant or broken and play space may be limited.

Questions: Here, observation, casual talk, and what-if questions are the key.

• *Talk about lifestyle. Find out the family's coming and goings, any stresses they may be experiencing.* This may feel like prying, but it's essential to know all you can about someone who'll care for your child.

• *How do the other kids look?* Do they seem happy and secure? Is there affection shown? How are conflicts handled? If the caregiver has her own children at home, observe their relationship.

• *Ask "What would you do if one child has a toy and my daughter grabs it from him and the first child hits her? . . . if my son empties your bedroom closet? . . . my baby is fussy and needs to be held for hours at a stretch?"* You may be confident that your child won't do any of the above; the point, however, is to get a sense of how naturally, sensitively, and intelligently the potential caregiver would respond. Certainly, if you have hit a snag in parenting, find out how your interviewee would handle it. At the very worst, you'll know what not to do.

• *Get the names of the other families that have used her home care, both children she now cares for and those who have "graduated."* Ask them about the caregiver's strengths and liabilities; how she handles illness and discipline; if she's affectionate and has stamina. If you really like someone, but have a specific concern, address it: "She seems to be a bit nervous. Is she overprotective with the children, or her house?" What's her turnover? Does she tend to have the same child for a few years indicating her good service?

Best for Baby

• *What will she feed your child?* White bread and butter may suit Little Tommy Tucker, but not today's tots. Unfortunately, to cut down on costs, some providers cut down on nutrition.

Cost: $1.50–$2.50 an hour, with lower rates for full-time children or two from one family. $50–$100 a week.

Parent Cooperative

As an alternative to these two most common options, some parents pool resources and start their own program. These range from two neighboring families who hire a "sitter" together, to ten families who hire two teachers, rent a space, and contribute work time.

Pros: The main advantage to this system is control. You choose the staff, facility, hours, and families. You make decisions, and friends. Parents learn a lot because of close relationships with caregivers and other co-op members. There is a high degree of parental involvement, giving that family feel, and these groups tend to have an unusually high proportion of men at the care site.

Cons: The main one is time. If you don't have some to spare, this may not be the option for you. Members usually commit to work time—at the center, in the office, or on various committees. Some co-ops allow members to put in more money in lieu of sweat.

Cost: This varies according to the space you use and your staff salaries. Child-care providers make a pitiful average of $8000 a year and are in the lowest 10% of wage earners in the country. In fact, we pay people more to take care of our pets. If you decide to go the co-op route, you can help to improve this situation.

Getting Ready

Whatever you choose for day care arrangements, prepare your child for what's to come. Preliminary visits, descriptions of a typical day, and picture books about day cares (we like Fred Roger's "Going to Day Care") and playgroups will give a toddler some sense of control in a new situation. For both infants and young toddlers, games of peek-a-boo (or for older ones, hide and seek) will help teach your baby that even when you disappear, you always come back.

Best for Baby

Childcare, International Style

As an answer to the need for quality, affordable infant day care, the advisory committee of the Yale Bush Center in Child Development and Social Policy recommends a six-month parental leave policy with reduced pay. After that leave, parents would be on their own. Here's how some countries handle this working parents' dilemma.

Sweden

New parents are entitled to one year of leave time. The first six months of this allottment may only be taken by the mother who receives 90% of her salary.

Denmark

New parents are entitled to a leave of twenty-four weeks. The first fourteen weeks of the leave are reserved for the mother. As compensation for a shorter leave than their Swedish neighbors, Denmark has a larger network of day-care facilities. Well over half the children under 5 are enrolled in public facilities for as low as $115 per month. Space availability for infants is so limited that municipalities pay women to watch two or three babies in their home.

France

Mothers receive sixteen weeks maternity leave at 84% of their salary. Approximately 1300 state-run centers, called crèches, can't keep up with the demand, so the government offers up to $340 per month to parents who hire someone to care for the baby in the family's home.

Japan

Mothers get fourteen weeks leave, but usually quit work to care for their babies. Social pressure is strong in Japan and society looks down on women who return to work. Most licensed centers won't take newborns and the government resists expansion to accommodate infants.

Israel

New mothers get twelve weeks paid leave and forty weeks unpaid. The 900 subsidized centers have a sliding fee scale and are overcrowded.

Soviet Union

New mothers get four months paid leave and are entitled to 25% of their salaries up until their child's first birthday. There is no paternity leave. Soviet nurseries are said to be poorly run, so most parents leave their children with grandma.

United States

Before their child's first birthday, 50% of new mothers return to work. Of working women in their child-bearing years, 93% expect to start families during their working years. The United States is the only western industrialized nation that doesn't guarantee a leave of absence after the birth of a child. Last January, the Supreme Court ruled that individual states may require businesses to grant such a leave. Currently 40% of U.S. women receive this leave and most leaves are brief and without pay. Of the nation's 6 million employers, 3000 provide some assistance, most in the form of referrals. Only 150 businesses provide on or near-site care, and the ones that do have received a lot of publicity.

The most progressive state in child-related services is Massachusetts. A comprehensive statewide referral network serves individuals and corporations. Small companies can get low-interest loans from the state to build facilities, and funds are allocated to start centers in housing projects. In 1987 the state spent about $27 million on day care and a total of $101 million on child-related services; it reports saving $121 million in welfare costs in 1986 alone.

Since 1981, much of the progress made in children's programs like general assistance efforts, food stamps, child welfare, etc. has been lost. Each year these programs have been cut back by $10 billion dollars. The closest we've come to a national day-care policy was in 1971 when Congress passed an amendment establishing a child day-care and development program. It was vetoed by President Nixon. The Child Welfare League of America is launching a twelve point platform on children as a major issue in the 1988 presidential campaign. The platform includes a provision for a child care policy.

Best Nannies

*Perhaps host and guest is
really the happiest relation for
father and son.*

Best Nannies

The first nannies as we know them came into existence in England during the late eighteenth century. Before that, the function of a nanny was wet nurse. Children of 300 to 400 years ago were sent out into the country to be suckled by foster mothers. They remained in such households until they were weaned and "trained" and returned to their real parents as late as age 5 or 6! The origin of the term *nanny*, which stems from this period, is obscure. Some historians attribute it to the Welsh word for grandma, which is identical.

During the eighteenth century, nannies began to move into the homes of their employers in the cities. Simultaneously, societal pressure was exerted on upper-class women to breastfeed their own children. Whether they breastfed or not, these women did tend to give over all other care of their offspring to a nanny. Nannies began to separate themselves from the rest of the domestic staff. They took their meals in the nursery. They often controlled all aspects of a child's life, including which schools they attended. More than one mother lived in fear of her children's nanny, deferring to her nanny's will even in obvious cases of mistreatment.

By the mid-nineteenth century, nannies had reached their golden epoch. A growing middle class bankrolled by the industrial revolution began to employ them. One estimates figures that between 1850 and 1939 well over 1 million women made their living this way. But the good old days came to an abrupt halt with the onset of World War II. Increasing taxation along with increasing wages for servants took their toll. All domestic employment, no matter the type, decreased drastically.

Today there is a resurgence of the nanny profession in the United States. Women are returning to professional careers after the births of their children. Nannies provide a measure of both flexibility and control not allowed by conventional day care. In many cases where a family can afford it, the nanny is the preferred childcare option.

The demand, unfortunately, has outstripped the supply. Today, nanny experts in this country estimate that between 10 and 250 positions are available for every qualified nanny applicant! Placement agencies from all over the United States have stories of receiving calls from all corners of the country, no matter how distant, from parents desperate to hire a qualified and experienced live-in caregiver. Many persons involved in nanny placement bemoan the Immigration Control & Reform Act passed by the 99th Congress in 1986. This law made it easier for illegal aliens here before January 1, 1982 to gain legal status, which was fine for nannies working here illegally at that time. But the new law also made it harder for anyone new to come in. Norland nannies, those legendary women trained at the Norland Nursery Training College in Berkshire, England, have become as rare as whooping cranes.

Still, Norland nannies set the standards by which all others are judged. Typical Norland training involves over 3900 hours of classroom and practical study, 85 written observations of different children, three months of hospital interning in maternity and sick children's wards, a passing grade on the National Nursery Examination Board's exam, and a nine-month probationary period that must end with a favorable report from their employer. Subjects of study include a thorough foray into child psychology, child illnesses, and first aid. Students also master such practical crafts as cooking, sewing, laundry, along with some more rarified ones like embroidery, smocking, and catering of children's birthday parties.

Best for Baby

Clearly, a school like Norland is the product of a long and august tradition of nannies. In this country we have no such heritage to draw on. Over fifty nanny training schools or programs have sprung up across the United States in recent years, but many are for profit. There is no national accrediting board that can judge them or establish minimum training requirements. Regulations to open a nanny program vary from state to state and in many cases involve nothing more than sending in a registration fee. Until such national standards have been set, the American parent must interview the school as well as the applicant. The recently formed International Nanny Association, based in California, is a nonprofit group attempting to bolster the quality of U.S. nanny training. Deborah Davis, the association's president, feels that a nanny's training should be even more rigorous than what is currently expected of group day-care employees, because a nanny is working with children in isolation.

The typical American nanny works five days a week, ten hours per day. They generally receive weekends off, two weeks paid vacation per year, major holidays, and extra pay for overtime. A separate nanny apartment is ideal, but at the very least they expect their own room and bath. Pay ranges from $150 to $400 per week, depending on experience and geographic location. California and the northeast tend to be the most expensive. Nannies also frequently receive health insurance from their employers.

Before hiring a nanny make sure that your child-rearing philosophies are compatible. Keep your relationship professional and respect your nanny's privacy and free time. Remember that a nanny is a professional and not you or your child's servant. If any issues arise, be sure to address them immediately.

A List of Nanny Training Programs

Note: * denotes a school widely considered to be first rate. † denotes a member of The American Council of Nanny Schools, a nonprofit organization that requires a minimum of 200 classroom and 50 field-work hours of its graduates and submission to curriculum review by other members.

Arizona

Development Center
  for Nannies
500 East Thomas
Phoenix, AZ 85012
(602) 279-3067
Training: 12-week program

California

† California Nanny College
  2740 Fulton Avenue   #129
  Sacramento, CA 95821
  (916) 484-0163
  Training: 15 weeks/600 hours

† The American Nanny Plan, Inc.
  P.O. Box 790
  Claremont, CA 91711
  (714) 625-7711

The Governess Agency/
  Governess Training Center
4655 Cass Street
San Diego, CA 92109
(619) 270-8311

American Nanny College
1268 North 2nd Street   Suite 2
El Cajon, CA 92021
(619) 470-9133
Training: 4-week program

The Nanny Institute, Inc.
6242 Plymouth
San Jose, CA 95129
(408) 257-0304

* Chaffee Community College
  Childhood Development
    Department
  5885 Haven Avenue
  Alta Loma, CA 91701
  (714) 987-1737
  *Training: 2-year degree
  program*

College of Siskiyous
800 College Avenue
Weed, CA 96094
(916) 938-4462

Grossmont College
Family and Consumer Studies
  Program
8800 Grossmont College Drive
El Cajon, CA
(619) 465-1700 Ex. 327

Los Medanos College
Pittsburg, CA 94565
(415) 439-2181

Colorado

National Academy of Nannies
3665 Cherry Creek Drive
  North   #320
Denver, CO 80209
(303) 333-NANI

Metropolitan State College
Early Childhood Education
Denver, CO 80204
(303) 629-3178

Florida

Nannies Training School, Inc.
6951 SW 134th Street
Miami, FL 33156
(305) 238-2988

Brevard Community College
Vocational Child Care
1519 Clearlake Road
Cocoa, FL 32922
(305) 632-1111

Georgia

The Original Nannies
   Unlimited
2300 Peachford Road
Atlanta, GA 30338
(404) 451-0936

Hawaii

Honolulu Community College
874 Dillingham Boulevard
Honolulu, Hawaii 96817
(808) 845-9104

Illinois

Nanny U
2253 Giddings
Chicago, IL 60625
(312) 334-2269

Iowa

Child Care Services
Kirkwood Community College
P.O. Box 2069
6301 Kirkwood Boulevard SW
Cedar Rapids, IA 52406
(319) 398-5411

Kansas

* Markham School for Nannies
14700 West Kellogg
Witchita, KS 67253
(316) 722-5660

Nanny International Training
   School & Placement
   Services, Inc.
501 East Pawnee Suite # 410
Wichita, KS 67211
(316) 265-5683

Dodge City Community College
2501 North 14th Avenue
Dodge City, KS 67801
(316) 225-1321
*Training: 1-year certificate
and 2-year degree programs*

Kentucky

* Midway College
Early Childhood Center
Midway, KY 40347
(606) 846-4421
*Training: 2-year program
including 6-month exchange
at Norland.*

Maine

Four Seasons Nanny School
P.O. Box 1208
Damariscotta, ME 04503
(207) 529-5720

Massachusetts

† New England School for Nannies
41 Baymor Drive
East Longmeadow, MA 01028

Professional Nannies, Inc.
345 Washington Street
Wellesley, MA 02181
(617) 237-0211

* The Child Care Institute
38 Pleasant Street   3rd Floor
Stoneham, MA 02180
(617) 279-0882

Michigan

† Nanny Academy of America, Inc.
171 Lakeshore Road
Grosse Point, MI 48236
(313) 884-7550

† Delta College Nanny
Training Program
University Center, MI 48170
(517) 686-9417

Minnesota

† Nanny Child Caring Plan, Inc.
5609 Lyndale Avenue South
Minneapolis, MN 55419
(612) 861-3389
(Associated with the Minneapolis Children's Medical Center)

Hennepin Technical Centers
North Campus
9000 7th Avenue North
Brooklyn Park, MN 53445
(612) 425-3800

Missouri

Southwest Missouri
State University
Home Economics Department
901 S. National   Box 104
Springfield, Missouri 65804
(417) 836-5880

Nebraska

† Bryan Nanny School
5000 Sumner Street
Lincoln, NB 68506
(402) 483-3801

New Hampshire

† St. Joseph Hospital School of
Health Occupations
5 Woodward Avenue
Nashua, NH 03061
(603) 882-3000

New Jersey

American Nanny Academy
179 Roselle Avenue West
Roselle Park, NJ 07204
(201) 494-2457

* Neighborhood Nannies, Inc.
203 King's Highway
East Haddonfield, NJ 08033
(609) 795-5833

New York

Career Specialist's Institute
3300 Munroe Avenue
Rochester, NY 14618
(716) 385-6556

Ohio

English Nannies School, Inc.
11125 Magnolia Drive/
University Circle
Cleveland, Ohio 44107
(216) 521-4650

* Nannies of Cleveland, Inc.
15707 Detroit Avenue
Lakewood, Ohio 44107
(216) 521-4650

† North American Nannies, Inc.
61 Jefferson Avenue
Columbus, Ohio 43215
(614) 228-6264

Oklahoma

† DeMarge Professional
Nanny Institute
3608 NW 58th Street
Oklahoma City, OK 73112
(405) 947-1534

Oregon

Nanny Academy Northwest
5188 SW Baird
Portland, OR 97219
(503) 244-0470

Northwest Nannies Institute
710 NE 21st Avenue
Portland, OR 97232
(503) 234-4671

* Lane Community College
4000 East 30th Avenue
Eugene, OR 97405
(503) 747-4501
*Training: 2-year degree
program*

Pennsylvania

Professional Child Care
299 Lancaster Avenue
Frazer, Pa
(215) 647-7195

Pennyslvania State University
410 Keller Conference Center
University Park, PA 16802
(814) 863-3551

* Community College of
Allegheny County, Center-North
1130 Perry Highway
Pittsburgh, PA 15237
(412) 734-4025
*Training: 1-year certificate
program, 2-year degree
program*

South Dakota

Aberdeen Academy of Nannies
406 Berkshire Plaza
Aberdeen, SD 54701
(605) 226-1817

Texas

Texas Academy of Nannies
P.O. Box 1058
Missouri City, TX 77849
(713) 696-8210

Brookhaven College
3939 Valley View Lane
Farmer's Branch, TX 75234
(214) 620-4130

Odessa College
Child Development
201 West University
Odessa, TX 79764

Virginia

Northern Virginia Community
   College
Early Childhood Education
3001 North Beauregard
Alexandria, VA 22311
(703) 845-6224

Washington

Certified Nanny Program
Seattle Central Community
   College
1701 Broadway
Seattle, WA 98122
(206) 587-6900

Wisconsin

University of Wisconsin—Stout
   Child Development Center
Menomonie, WI 54751
*Training: Very comprehensive
program*

A List of
Nanny Agencies

Alaska

Professional Rent-a Mom
(Anchorage)
(907) 349-2331 or 349-4463

Arizona

Domestic Consultants, Inc.
(Scottsdale)
(602) 941-5150
Attention Unlimited (Phoenix)
(602) 978-2306

California

Au Pair Connection
(Huntington Beach)
(714) 964-5231

Be In Our Care Agency
(Walnut Creek)
(415) 933-2273

Bananas
(Oakland)
(415) 658-7101

Here's Help, Inc.
(San Francisco)
(415) 931-4357

June Art Agency
(Beverly Hills)
(213) 273-5655

Naturally Nannies Agency
(San Diego)
(619) 268-8030

Northern California Nannies
   Agency, Inc.
(Los Altos)
(415) 949-2933

Sandra Taylor Agency
(Beverly Hills)
(213) 278-7535

Nannies and Grannies
(Orange)
(714) 997-2500

Colorado

Child Care Connections
(Denver)
(303) 825-7141

Starkey & Associates
(Denver)
(303) 394-4904

Connecticut

A Child's Care Inc.
(Ridgefield)
(203) 431-8991

HELP!
(Weston)
(203) 226-3456

Helping Hands
(Wilton)
(203) 834-1742

Overseas Maid Service
(Stamford)
(203) 324-7595

Sitting Pretty
(Guilford)
(203) 453-3233

Nannies Across America
(Stamford)
(203) 359-3071

Nannies Unlimited
(Guilford)
(203) 453-6664

District of Columbia

Help Is On the Way, Inc.
(202) 488-3445

Kidpanions
(301) 657-3583

Nanny Placement Services
(202) 342-1405

Florida

Nanny Placement Service
(Ft. Lauderdale)
(305) 975-5443

Georgia

Nannies Unlimited
(404) 451-0936

Nanny Pop-Ins, Inc.
(404) 399-6186

Idaho

National Nannies
(Boise)
(208) 345-3051

Illinois

Naperville Nannies, Inc.
(Naperville)
(312) 357-0808

Kansas

Midwest Nannies
(Witchita)
(316) 721-1904

Nannies of Kansas City, Ltd.
(Prairie Village)
(913) 341-6447

Maine

Portland Nannies
(Portland)
(207) 77C-HILD

Maryland

Modern Nanny, Inc.
(Gaithersberg)
(301) 869-6461

Massachusetts

Child Care Management
(Needham)
(617) 444-4880

Child Care Placement Service
(Brookline)
(617) 566-6294

The Child Care Connection
(Wellesley Hills)
(617) 237-7330

American Au Pair
(Boston)
(617) 244-5154

Nanny Service
(Worcester)
(617) 755-9284

Rent-a-Nanny
(Peabody)
(617) 535-3577

The Child Care Institute
(Stoneham)
(617) 922-0526

The Helping Hand
(Beverly Hills)
(617) 922-0526

One on One, Inc.
(Andover)
(617) 794-2035

Minnesota

Granny's Nannies
(Brainerd)
(218) 828-4289

Nannyfinders
(Brooklyn Park)
(612) 924-6404

National Nanny Resource and
    Referral
(Minneapolis)
(612) 566-1561

Missouri

Annie's Nannies
(Clayton)
(314) 727-ANNY

Nannies by Nita
(St. Louis)
(314) 644-4024

Gingerbread Nannies
(Springfield)
(417) 88N-ANNY

Montana

Nannies Preferred
(Great Falls)
(406) 727-6708

Quality Placements
(Great Falls)
(406) 453-6814

Best for Baby

Nebraska

My Nanny, Inc.
(Omaha)
(402) 978-3412

New Jersey

Domestic Connection
(201) 984-2440

Nannies Plus
(201) 535-5838

National Nanny Network
(Rivervale)
(210) 358-1613

Good Help, Inc.
(Sparta)
(201) 729-HELP

Apple Pie, Inc.
(Upper Montclair)
(201) 746-7813

Caregivers, Inc.
(201) 272-3180

Child Care Resources, Inc.
(609) 683-9595

Children's Services of Morris
  County
(Mt. Freedom)
(201) 895-2676

New York

Career Specialists Institute
(Rochester)
(716) 385-3180

New York Link
(Albany)
(518) 472-1522

Rent-a-Mom
(Liverpool)
(315) 451-0993

The Fox Agency
(New York)
(212) 753-2686

Child Care Decisions, Inc.
(Pleasantville)
(914) 747-0264

Domestic Solutions, Inc.
(Baldwin)
(516) 223-3600

Mornings 'R Us
(Nesconset)
(516) 360-3250

Nannies of New York, Inc.
(Garden City)
(516) 484-9180

Professional Nannies Institute
(New York)
(212) 692-9510

Robin Kellner Agency
(New York)
(516) 627-4678

Take Care, Inc.
(New York)
(212) 262-5155

Arlene Streisand, Inc.
(New York)
(800) 443-6428

North Carolina

Nanny Finders, Inc.
(Chapel Hill)
(919) 968-8789

Nanny's Here, Ltd.
(Clemmons)
(916) 766-4439

More than Nannies, Inc.
(Durham)
(919) 544-4448

Ohio

Apple of Your Eye
(Cincinnati)
(513) 530-0999

Oregon

Moore's Nanny Agency
(Roseburg)
(503) 673-0064

Pennsylvania

Domestic Employment Service
(Jenkintown)
(215) 885-6875

Professional Child Care
(Frazer)
(215) 647-7195

Renee Miller Agency
(Philadelphia)
(215) 877-1183

The Philadelphia Nanny Network
(Philadelphia)
(215) 546-3002

Rent-a-Mom
(Wexford)
(412) 935-0455

Rhode Island

Progressive Nannies, Inc.
(401) 946-0850

Professional Nanny School of
   Rhode Island
(Narragansett)
(401) 783-0070

The Nanny Connection of
   Rhode Island
(Pawtucket)
(401) 724-2743

South Carolina

The Nanny Connection
(Summerville)
(803) 875-1997

Nannies, Inc.
(Columbia)
(803) 254-9264

Texas

Moms, Inc.
(Houston)
(713) 999-8800

The Nanny Company
(Austin)
(512) 459-2200

The Professional Nanny of Dallas,
   Inc.
(Dallas)
(214) 661-1296

Utah

Nanny Placement Services,
International, Inc.
(Salt Lake City)
(801) 538-2122

Dial-a-Nanny
(Salt Lake City)
(801) 943-4434

Virginia

Nanny Connections
(Fairfax)
(703) 352-4581

Neighborhood Nannies, Ltd.
(Arlington)
(703) 276-8979

Mothers-in-Deed
(Arlington)
(703) 920-2454

Washington

Annie's Nannies
(Seattle)
(206) 784-8462

Mrs. B's Nanny Referrals
(Spokane)
(509) 325-2197

Nannies Nationwide, Inc.
(Seattle)
(206) 283-5107

Northwest Nannies, Inc.
(Bellevue)
(206) 453-7289

Best for Baby

Questions for a Prospective Nanny

What is your academic background in child care?

Can you document it?

Describe your training.

What do you feel are the particular daily duties of a nanny?

Have you had any long-term contact giving care to children? Do you have a reference from this experience?

How long would you like to work as a nanny?

Do you have a clean driving record?

Do you have any emergency medical training like C.P.R.?

What is your child-rearing philosophy?

Is this the way you were raised? How is it different?

Do you have any chronic physical problems that may interfere with your child-care responsibilities?

Describe some difficult on-the-job situations. How did you handle them?

What did you like or dislike about previous jobs?

Do you smoke or drink? Will it offend you if we do?

Agency Questions

How long have you been in business?

Are you licensed? What are the state license requirements?

Where do you find your applicants?

What is your screening process? Will you conduct an FBI check if I'd like one?

What percentage of applicants do you turn away?

Can you refer satisfied former customers?

Will you replace a nanny who isn't working out?

What are your fees?

Note: Some agencies bond, insure, and pay their nannies directly and you pay the agency. If you pay your nanny directly, check with your accountant about social security deductions, unemployment taxes, and so forth.

Miscellaneous

Health Insurance

Your nanny can join the National Association for the Education of Young Children and receive group health through them. Their address:
   1834 Connecticut Avenue, NW
   Washington, DC 20009
   (800) 424-2460

Au Pair/Homestay USA

This new program of the U.S. Information Agency is administered by the Experiment in International Living. The Experiment selects young adults from Europe who wish to live with a U.S. family for one year in return for child care. The au pairs are from 18 to 25 years of age and come primarily from Germany, England, Denmark, Switzerland, and Holland. They speak English, are of good character, and undergo a thorough medical exam before coming. They also receive health and accident insurance through the program. The program is well outlined with careful specifics of what is expected on both ends. The all-inclusive costs including $100-per-week allowance, interview fees, and a small tuition subsidy should your au pair opt for it are approximately $8000 annually. The Experiment is a wonderful liason officer and organizes frequent get-togethers for the au pairs in your area thereby avoiding the most common au pair problem: loneliness. For more information contact:
   Au Pair/Homestay USA
   The Experiment in International
      Living
   Suite 1100
   1522 K Street NW
   Washington, DC 20077
   (202) 371-9410

The National Nanny Newsletter

This piece is published under the auspices of the International Nanny Association mentioned earlier. It comes out four times a year, contains a wide variety of articles by and for nannies and nanny families, and has a want-ad section. $16 per year. Contact:
   National Nanny Newsletter
   976 Foothill Boulevard Suite 591
   Claremont, CA 91711

Further Reading

The best book we've found on nannies is *The Nanny Connection: How to Find and Keep a Perfect Nanny* by Robin Sweet and Mary Ellen Siegal, Atheneum, paperback, $7.95.

Special Products for
Premature Infants

Special Products for Premature Infants

In the United States, over 250,000 babies are born prematurely every year. These premature infants fall into two groups. Near-term infants may remain a few days in an incubator. But children who weigh under 3 pounds when born may spend weeks or even months in the neonatal intensive-care ward of the nearest research hospital. One thing all preemies have in common is the need for special care.

A number of companies have designed special products for these special infants. Since a premature birth is often a surprise, leaving new parents little time to prepare, we have organized this section around suppliers that will respond immediately by mail or by phone to your needs.

Parent Care

This is a nonprofit, international organization that offers information, referrals, and other services to families, support groups, and professionals involved with infants who require intensive or special care at birth. They publish a quarterly newsletter and offer regional conferences in addition to an annual international conference. For the $25 membership fee, parents receive a copy of their comprehensive resource directory, the newsletter, and special rates to regional conferences.

Parent Care, Inc.
University of Utah Health
  Sciences
Room 2A 210
50 North Medical Drive
Salt Like City, UT 84132

Best for Baby

Clothing

Preemies by Penguinie

A former registered nurse whose friend gave birth to a premature baby created this company. Today she offers a full line of preemie clothing from sleepers to outer garments. She even offers hand-knit sweaters. There is a three-day turnaround from the time she receives your check (all clothing is made to order and she is happy to comply with your fabric and color preferences).

Preemies by Penguinie
3009 North River Drive
Algonquin, IL 60102
(312) 658-9374
(24-hour answering)

Little Me for Preemies

The Schwab Company makes this line of preemie infant clothing. They focus on a baby's layette. Items are available in 100% cotton inter-lock weave or 100% polyester. They are available at the top department stores and baby shops around the country. ***Prices range from $7 to $20 per garment.*** For the store nearest you call Jamie Jordan at (301) 729-4488, or write The Schwab Company, Upper Potomac Industrial Park, Cumberland, Maryland 21501-1742.

Diapers

Preemie Pampers

These disposables can be ordered by phoning the Procter & Gamble company directly at 1-800-543-4932. They come 180 to the case. Procter & Gamble accepts Mastercard and Visa over the phone or will mail them out C.O.D. *Retail price: $20.50 per case by credit card, or $22.40 if shipped C.O.D.*

Preemie Pals

This cottage business manufactures fitted cloth diapers for infants between 4 and 10 pounds. The diapers are made of six layers of soft white flannel, a fabric preferred for its absorption and durability. They also sell preemie plastic pants that are machine washable. The owner will ship the diapers the next business day after receipt of your check. *Diapers are $15 per dozen. Plastic pants are $2 each.*

Preemie Pals
Nancy Nelson
1313 Harrison Avenue, S.E.
Renton, Washington 98058
(206) 271-0423

Feeding Gear

Remond Preemie Nipple

Remond is a line of *top*-quality nipples and bottles imported from France. They manufacture a special preemie nipple for newborns that is smaller and softer than a regular one. It features the Remond ogival shape, a reverse curve that allows the baby to breathe without difficulty. Air regulators, which allow air into the bottle, prevent aerophagia. The regulator can also be tightened to control liquid flow. All their nipples are 100% pure rubber. They can be ordered from their importer, Handy Chair, by calling 1-800-426-9244, or writing The Handy Chair Corporation, 307 19th Street, Lynden, WA 98264. Handy usually ships the same day they receive your order. *A package of two nipples sells for $2.*

Miscellaneous

Ride Rite

Although this car-seat cushion receives mention in the car-seat section, we think it merits special notice here. Doctors at the University of Nebraska have discovered that it is extremely dangerous to have preemies ride in car seats. Their necks are often still unable to support their heads at an angle that guarantees an open windpipe. The **Ride Rite** is designed for newborns in general but is a must for especially small infants. Be sure to consult your doctor *whether or not it is safe to use a car seat at all*, and if it is, whether they recommend the **Ride Rite**. *Approximate Retail: $12.95.* See car-seat section for production information.

Best for Baby

Books

Highly Recommended

The Premature Baby Book by Helen Harrison with Ann Kositsky, R.N., St. Martin's Press, 1983, $15.95

This book is frequently given by neonatal wards to the new parents of a premature infant. The author is the parent of a preemie. She goes in depth into the basic medical information on prematurity. She discusses preemie infants' most frequent conditions and their underlying physiology. The book also includes a thorough and complete section on taking your premature infant home. Interwoven throughout are profiles of emotional responses by parents of newborn preemies. The books concludes with a good appendix of resources of both products and information.

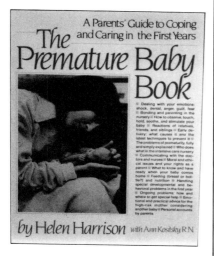

Also recommended

The Preemie Parents' Handbook by Adrienne B. Lieberman and Thomas G. Sheagren, Dutton, $10.95

This book emphasizes the parents' role in bearing and caring for a premature infant. There's a good discussion of doctor-parent communication. It also has a very fine section on breastfeeding. The authors discuss in great detail what your preemie will be like at home, and they finish with information on subsequent pregnencies, always a topic of concern. $10.95

Premature Babies, A Handbook For Parents by Sherri Nance, Arbor House, $15.95, Berkley, $4.50.

This book is possibly the first written on premature infants. It is emotionally oriented and focuses on this part of the experience over the more nuts-and-bolts medical aspects. It contains a resource section, an appendix on sewing preemie clothes, and the results of a study of 100 preemie parents. Nance has a comforting and warm tone.

Born Early, The Story of a Premature Baby by Mary Ellen Avery, M.D. and Georgia Litwack, Little Brown, $15.95.

This is the uplifting story of Adrienne Weber, a baby born at 1 pound 9 ounces and her victorious struggle to survive. It is filled with pictures and discusses the development of a preemie in the context of one baby's experience.

Best Miscellany

Best for Baby

Bow Back Rocker

A frequently overlooked necessity for a new nursery is a comfortable place for nursing or comforting mothers and fathers to sit. Many people with experience recommend a rocking chair—restful for parents' backs and soothing to baby. The elegant, classic lines of the **Bow Back Rocker** pictured above lend to almost all interiors. It is manufactured by Chatham County from steambent beechwood. The rocker comes in white or natural finishes, both nontoxic. It is also widely available at baby stores. *Approximate retail: $240.*

Ride Rite

A problem for all new parents transporting a really young infant in a car seat is head and neck support. The answer to this problem is the **Ride Rite** car seat cushion by Pansy Ellen. The specially contoured nonallergenic foam correctly positions a newborn in the car seat for a safe and comfortable ride. It also helps lift harness straps away from your baby's face. The cushion covering is terrycloth next to the baby's skin, with the rest a poly-cotton. It removes easily for washing and fits all federally approved car seats. The **Ride Rite** will fit an infant weighing up to 15 pounds. *Approximate retail: $12.95.*

Auto Sun Shade

Another item to make your new baby's car rides more comfortable is the **Sun Shade Kit** by Prince Lionheart. It is a smoke-colored, see-through vinyl sheet, 16 × 22 inches, that adheres to a car window by means of static cling. The **Sun Shade** comes with a foam sponge to create static and a squeegee to remove air bubbles. The vinyl is treated to block out most ultraviolet rays. Best of all, it comes in a neat reusable plastic box that fits in a glove compartment. A must for long trips or summer babies. *Approximate retail: $5.00.*

TenderTouch

Infant massage is a recent popular and positive form of parent and child interaction. **TenderTouch** is a 28-minute color video on the subject designed to teach the fundamentals. It has 22 minutes of massage instruction covering thirty-two separate strokes plus a question-and-answer period. The video is led by Sandra Truxell, a registered nurse and massage therapist who has worked in obstetrics for seventeen years. She has taught massage as a part of routine obstetrical care for the last four. Studies have indicated that preemies treated with massage show superior growth and development. Comments from parents of full birth-weight babies assert that their infants really love it. For working parents, it can help bring you closer to baby after a hectic day and will probably calm you both. *Retail price, Beta or VHS format: $29.95.*

Gerry Deluxe Baby Monitor

When it comes to helping you utilize those precious free moments during young infant care, this **Deluxe Baby Monitor** made by Gerry can save the day. The FM transmitter with monitor microphone plugs into an outlet near the child for a strong, clear signal that lets you work in another part of the house, or even outdoors and keep listening in. The portable receiver can be carried or clipped onto your belt letting you roam up to 300 feet away. The long external an-

tenna helps ensure clear reception. The receiver operates on one 9-volt battery and comes with an AC adapter to prolong battery life, as well as a limited one-year warranty. Underwriter's Laboratory listed and FCC approved. This item is part of Gerry's Baby Safetronics line. They've recently added a two-way nursery intercom that's great for older children. *Approximate retail: $40.*

Best for Baby

Bath Center

The **Bath Center** is another product by Fisher-Price that rises above its competitors because of innovative but eminently practical design. This little tub fits in all sinks, double or single. The wide and deep washing area is covered by a mildew-resistant foam pad. A drain plug in the bottom makes it easy to avoid messy spills. The rinse pitcher and soap dish that fit neatly into the frame can be snapped together to make a tugboat with squeaker once your baby has moved to a full-sized tub. The **Bath Center** comes in a cheery royal blue and weighs 1½ pounds dry. *Approximate retail: $14.*

Little Potty

Another Swedish import by Baby Björn, this clear toddler potty was originally designed for Swedish day-care centers so that supervisors could monitor a number of trainees at once. What they discovered in the process was that children on the clear potties became toilet-trained faster. Educators believe (or maybe guess is a better word) that it's because they can *see* what they're doing, and make the connection more quickly. The **Little Potty** meets our standard for practicality because it's so simple to clean. *Note*: this potty is smaller than many on the market and therefore totes beautifully. Also available in light blue, pink, and white (for two dollars less). *Approximate retail: $16.*

Fisher-Price Potty

The manufacturer claims that this potty is the first designed for all three stages of toilet training. For "rookies" there's the free-standing potty seat with removable pot. The "trainee" seat removes to be placed on top of adult toilet seats and the pot flips over to be used as a stool. For "veterans" there is the stool by itself, useful when a child has adapted to a full-sized seat but still has trouble reaching it. When veterans no longer need the stool, veterans' parents usually nab it to be used for years throughout the rest of the house. The potty is made of durable, easy-to-clean plastic and comes with a training booklet. *Approximate retail: $16.*

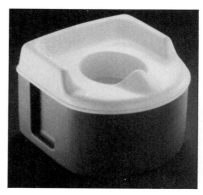

Bathe & Change

In the fifties, bathinettes were very popular. Today they have all but disappeared. In comes Baby Björn presenting the **Bathe & Change**, an updated version that we love. The white plastic unit is designed to fit directly over a bathtub. Its diaper changing surface lifts up to reveal a blue vinyl baby-sized bathtub. You fill the tub with a hand-held shower and let the water drain through a plastic tube directly into your tub or shower when bathtime is over. Shelves underneath and two organizers alongside contain lots of space for diapers, towels, and soap. Nicest of all, it can be easily closed up for storage, a terrific space saver for tiny apartments. *Approximate retail: $180.*

Kindergard Child Safety Products

One friend of ours reports that he covered all sharp corners in his house with halves of tennis balls to prevent toddler mishaps. Kindergard, the leader in the child safety products field, markets products that gracefully surpass such improvisations. Their line originated with clear plastic cabinet latches. (When their product was first introduced, there were 500,000 child poisonings annually. Today, 100 million latches later, that number has been reduced to 200,000.) They followed with Outlet Plugs, Edge and Corner Cushions, Doorknob Guards, and Electrical Cord Shorteners just to name a few. They are a company genuinely dedicated to a child's well-being. All products are manufactured in the United States under strict quality control and double inspections. Their line is widely available and items *retail for between $3 and $8.*

Safeguard 285 Vaporizer

Sixty-three years ago, Kaz invented the vaporizer and today they still head the market. Recent technological improvements make their vaporizers safer and silent too. The **Safeguard 285** has triple-wall construction. Special vents regulate steam and prevent overboiling. The nonrust, noncorrosive carbon electrodes work with all types of tap water. The 2-gallon tank generates steam for up to 24 hours and comes with an automatic shut-off and night light. *Note:* Vaporizers are recommended by almost all doctors for upper respiratory illnesses in infants and children. *Approximate retail: $19 to $22.*

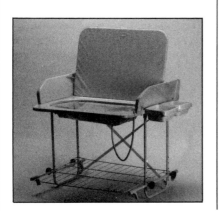

Adjustable Guard Rail

This sturdy, lightweight guard rail is excellent for toddlers making the switch to a full-sized bed. The plastic is nontoxic and the legs are designed fit under the mattress without slipping. The guard rail adjusts from 43 to 59 inches in length and is 16 inches tall. It can be pulled apart for storage or travel. Available in red, blue, beige, white, light blue, and pink by Dmka. *Approximate retail: $20.*

Nu-Line Pressure Gate 202

Another item useful for growing children is a safety gate. The **Nu-Line 202** consistently tests out highest among pressure-mounted gates. (Permanent gates are generally stronger, but many people object to the damage to the woodwork caused by mounting them directly into doorframes.) It has a wood frame and plastic mesh covering. The gate adjusts from 27½ to 42 inches wide and is 24 inches high, low enough for most adults to step over. This particular model is the best-selling safety gate in the country, but Nu-Line has a large selection of gates to choose from. *Approximate retail: $10 to $12.*

Splat Mat

Once you reach your destination, especially if it's Grandma's, you will definitely score points by bringing along a **Splat Mat**. This 3 × 4 foot heavy-duty vinyl mat will protect 12 square feet from baby's spills and splashes. If you're faced with strained beet stains, this is no small achievement. The **Splat Mat** is tough but soft. A simple silk-screened pattern designed to blend with most decors is printed in nontoxic ink. It folds down to 6 × 9 inches for storage. *Approximate retail: $8.95.*

Best Schools

Best Schools

Traditionally, credit goes to Boston Latin School, founded in 1634, for being the first and oldest elementary school in the United States. But in reality, the first schools in this country were set up by Franciscan friars along the Rio Grande in 1582 to convert the Indians to Catholicism. Fifty years later, their Protestant neighbor to the northeast founded schools along similar religious lines. The Puritan General Court of Massachusetts Bay Colony ordered schools into existence in 1642 to counteract the effects of "that Old Deluder Satan." It required all parents and masters with apprentices to make sure their young charges could read the Scriptures and follow catechisms. Apparently the response to this edict was too slack, so in 1647 the court established fines for towns of 50 or more families who failed to hire and support a teacher. Towns of 100 families were required to set up an establishment for a Latin master as well.

Religious studies dominated schooling well into the eighteenth century. At the same time, leaders like Benjamin Franklin had begun to agitate for a wider and more practical range of school subjects. Franklin harbored a keen admiration for the fictional hero Robinson Crusoe, who used his hands as well as his mind to survive. Even with all his persuasive charm, however, Franklin failed to make much of a dent in educational attitudes during his lifetime. Religious educational ideals prevailed and most citizens of the new republic still held study of Latin and the ancient Greeks as the only worthwhile education.

It took the industrial revolution and a strengthening democracy in the nineteenth century to make significant change. It was a century of education landmarks. In 1821, the first free high school, Boston English High School, opened. Horace Mann campaigned for and was hugely successful in introducing a more universal and secular mode of school. He also introduced the organizational idea of formal grades with certain requirements to pass from one to the next. Labor unions began to demand free public education for their workers' children. Spelling, grammar, and geography were added to the three R's as standard subjects to study by midcentury, and the 1880s saw U.S. history added to the list. In fact, the century was an unqualified leap forward in almost all ways but one: the caliber of most teachers, especially on the elementary school level, was astoundingly poor. By 1904, less than half had completed a high school education. High schools fared better—most teachers there had finished high school, and many had even gone to college.

In our century, many earlier educational gains have consolidated. By 1920, not only was free public schooling universal, but every state finally had a compulsory attendance law. Teacher education standards were set. All teachers now complete a college degree, and many have a graduate degree as well. The list of available subjects has continuously lengthened to the point where many parents today are worried that the basic skills are being overlooked. We've added nursery schools and kindergartens, junior high schools and junior colleges.

School enrollment shot up during the baby boom following World War II and shrunk when the boomers entered the workforce. Recently, a sizeable Hispanic population pressing for bilingual education has created controversy and new challenges in several urban areas. In the eighties, alarming reports about widespread illiteracy have helped make education a key topic on the political and personal agenda once again. In our opinion, it's never too soon to start mulling over your education options.

Top Public Schools

Until recently, it was difficult to pinpoint the outstanding public schools across the nation. Unlike private institutions, public schools are handed their student bodies, and in all but a few cases must do nothing to attract them. In 1986, the U.S. Department of Education inaugurated a recognition program. They named 270 public and private (read parochial) schools across the country as outstanding examples of places where students "develop a strong core of skills and knowledge, good values and habits, and an enthusiastic attitude toward learning." Over 500 schools were nominated by the chief state school officer in each state and the District of Columbia. The final group was selected by an appointed group of educators, state officials, and private citizens. They intend to update the list in alternating years. You may obtain a free copy of the list by writing:

School Recognition Program
U.S. Department of Education
555 New Jersey Avenue
  NW/Room 508
Washington, D.C. 20208

Best for Baby

Top Private Elementary Schools

All schools are K–12 and co-ed, unless otherwise noted.

Arizona
Phoenix Country Day School (Phoenix)
Tennis courts, palm trees, a wide variety of subjects, and the reputation for a caring faculty.

California
Chadwick School (Palos Verdes Peninsula)
Rigorous academics in a halcyon setting; strong commitment to community service.

La Jolla Country Day (La Jolla)
Generally considered the best school in the San Diego area. Excellent college placement.

Polytechnic School (Pasadena)
East coast prep school academics in a California setting. Tough to get in. Excellent college placement.

Connecticut
Hopkins Grammar/Day Prospect Hill School (New Haven)
Even though they start with seventh grade, they're worth mentioning as the oldest private day school in the country. A lovely setting. Half the senior class are usually National Merit finalists.

Greens Farms Academy (Greens Farms)
All girls. Snobbish and genuinely good academics.

Delaware
Wilmington Friends School (Wilmington)
Politically aware student body. Obligatory course in non-violence.

District of Columbia
Georgetown Day School
A progressive school with fine academics. Less fine athletics. Lots of politically oriented extracurriculars.

National Cathedral School
All girls. Competitive academic program oriented to the Ivy League.

St. Albans School
All boys. Widely considered to be D.C.'s toniest school. Probably D.C.'s smartest student body as well.

The Sidwell Friends School
Strong girls' teams. Liberal orientation. Good school newspaper.

Hawaii
Iolani School (Honolulu)
Excellent program in math and sciences. A block from Waikiki Beach.

St. Andrew's Priory School (Honolulu)
All girls. Strong academics.

Illinois
University of Chicago Laboratory School (Chicago)
Students have access to all university facilities. Excellent college placement.

Indiana
Park Tudor School (Indianapolis)

Kansas
Wichita Collegiate School (Wichita)

Maryland
Gilman School (Baltimore)
Innovative attitudes for such a strong academic environment.

The Holton-Arms School (Bethesda)
All girls. Begins with third grade. Competes with the best nationally.

The Park School (Brookland-ville)
They have a policy of no rules to help foster student maturity. Amazingly, it works.

Roland Park Country Day School (Baltimore)
All girls, traditional and sophisticated.

Massachusetts
Buckingham, Brown and Nichols School (Cambridge)
Diverse student body with a lively academic program.

Milton School (Milton)
Top-notch

Michigan
Detroit Country Day School (Birmingham)
Most desirable in the area.

Minnesota
Blake's School (Minneapolis)
Strong athletics

St. Paul Academy and Summit School (St. Paul)
Great academics in good surroundings

Missouri
Mary Institute (St. Louis)
All girls. Preppie.

New Jersey
Montclair-Kimberly (Montclair)

Princeton Day School (Princeton)
A strong student body. A planetarium and hockey rink are among the facilities.

New York
Albany Academy (Albany)
All boys.

Albany Academy for Girls (Albany)

The Brearly School (New York)
Very stiff admissions standards.

The Chapin School (New York)
Tough to get in, but the academic program isn't good enough to justify such difficult admission. All girls.

Collegiate School (New York)
Ten years older than Harvard. Excellent academics.

The Dalton School (New York)
Diverse student body enthusiastically pursuing strong academic program.

Fieldston School (Bronx)

Friends Academy (Locust Valley)
One of the best on Long Island.

Friends Seminary (New York)

The Horace Mann–Barnard School (Bronx)
Some say this is the best elementary school in the country.

Riverdale Country Day School (Bronx)
Not as good as it once was, but still strong.

Rye Country Day School (Rye)

St. Ann's School (Brooklyn)
No grades, only progress reports. Liberal, lively student body.

The Spence School (New York)
All girls. Very social.

Trinity School (New York)
Great facilities and academics.

Woodmere Academy (Woodmere)

North Carolina
Cape Fear Academy (Wilmington)
Small classes. Outstanding athletics.

Durham Academy (Durham)

Greensboro Day School (Greensboro)
Reputation for a fine faculty.

Best for Baby

Ohio

Cincinnati Country Day School (Cincinnati)

Columbus Academy (Gahanna)

The Columbus School for Girls (Columbus)

Hawken School (Gates Mills)

Miami Valley School (Dayton)

Oklahoma

Casady School (Oklahoma City)

Heritage Hall (Oklahoma City)

Pennsylvania

The Agnes Irwin School (Rosemont)
All girls. Highly respected academically. Outstanding dance program.

Chestnut Hill Academy (Philadelphia)
Pools its resources with Springside School (all girls) for a wonderful example of co-operative education.

The Ellis School (Pittsburgh)
All girls.

Friends Central School (Philadelphia)
Narrow course offering but what they offer is the best.

Germantown Friends School (Philadelphia)

The Haverford School (Haverford)
All boys.

The Shipley School (Bryn Mawr)

William Penn Charter School (Philadelphia)
Co-ed till the sixth grade, all boys thereafter.

Rhode Island

Lincoln School (Providence)
All girls.

Moses Brown School (Providence)
Quaker with strong program in both athletics and academics.

South Carolina

Porter-Gaud School (Charleston)
One of the best in the South.

Tennessee

University School of Nashville (Nashville)
Liberal. Wide course selection.

Texas

Greenhill School (Dallas)

The Kincaid School (Houston)

St. John's School (Houston)
Stiff admissions.

St. Mark's School of Texas (Dallas)
All boys.

Virginia

Norfolk Academy (Norfolk)
A bit regimented.

St. Anne's–Belfield School (Charlottesville)
Well-rounded course offering.

St. Christopher's School (Richmond)
All boys.

Washington

The Bush School (Seattle)
Great school that is experientially oriented. Wonderful and popular faculty.

Charles Wright Academy (Tacona)
Emphasis on the individual student.

Alternative Philosophies: Montessori and Waldorf Schools

Waldorf Schools

Rudolph Steiner founded the first Waldorf school in Stuttgart, Germany in 1919. Its innovative educational methods soon aroused interest. A Waldorf education aims to strengthen moral, artistic, and intellectual abilities equally, not one at the expense of the others. Piaget and others have confirmed the effectiveness of this approach in research studies.

The Waldorf curriculum is broad and balanced and includes humanities, arts, and sciences. In preschool the emphasis is on hands-on activity. In elementary school the emphasis is more on a child's emotional and artistic development. Finally, high school emphasizes the rapidly unfolding intellect.

Today there are over 350 Waldorf schools on five continents, and a number of teacher training centers. You can find out more about this innovative educational philosophy and whether there is a Waldorf school near you by writing:

Mrs. Anne Charles
Association of Waldorf Schools of
North America
17 Hemlock Hill
Great Barrington, MA 01230

Montessori Schools

Dr. Maria Montessori developed her revolutionary ideas about children and their education at the beginning of this century. Since then her philosophy has caught on around the world. Her educational system is child-centered as opposed to teacher-centered. Montessori believed that children learn and achieve discipline naturally if they are placed in an aesthetically pleasant environment with an ordered arrangement of sequential learning materials that are developmentally appropriate. A Montessori environment is noncompetitive and allows a child to proceed at his or her own pace and motivation. Judging from the response of parents and teachers of nursery-educated Montessori students, her methods work beautifully. The Montessori method is by no means limited to preschool age children, though, even if she did believe the years up to age 6 were most important. For more information about Montessori methods and schools near you contact:

The American Montessori Society
150 Fifth Avenue
New York, NY 10011
(212) 924-3209

Best for Baby

Education and Supplements

Outward Bound

Dr. Kurt Hahn, a German educator fleeing the Nazis, began Outward Bound in Wales in 1941. His philosophy was to use the wilderness as a medium to learn about the self. His main lesson was to teach his participants that most limits are self-imposed. His philosophy carries over today in courses offered around the world that teach self-confidence through teamwork as well as respect for the environment and community. There are five Outward Bound schools in the United States alone; they teach and administer over 500 courses annually in twenty different states. Courses can be attended by persons aged 14 and up. They also offer special multi-element courses for groups of 14 to 16 year olds only. A typical course is the fourteen-day trip run by Colorado Outward Bound on the Green River that includes rafting, backpacking, rock climbing, and canyon exploration. Inclusive cost: $995. For more information write or call:

Outward Bound USA
National Headquarters
384 Field Point Road
Greenwich, CT 06830
(203) 661-0797

Earthwatch

This nonprofit organization finds volunteers for academically oriented research expeditions in a wide variety of fields like archeology, primatology, marine studies, ecology, and public health. A typical offering is their current archeological expedition in Tierra del Fuego called "Sub-Arctic Fisher-men." Scientists are investigating the Fuegian people's switch from a hunter-gatherer to a sea-harvesting culture, then comparing their data to other well-studied groups from similar climates. A two-week stint costs $1575 plus air fare and is tax-deductible. Some student and teacher scholarships are available. Contact:

Earthwatch
680 Mt. Auburn Street
Box 403
Watertown, MA 05673
(617) 926-8200

Special Students

Council for Exceptional Students
1920 Association Drive
Reston, VA 22901
(703) 620-3660

This organization of educational professionals provides information to parents, professionals, policy makers, and librarians about programs and resources for gifted as well as handicapped children. They can send you a series of fact sheets and reading lists, as well as refer you to various state agencies for further help.

National Information Center for
  Handicapped Children and Youth
P.O. Box 1492
Washington, D.C. 20013

NICHY is a free information service that assists educators, parents, caregivers, and others in ensuring that all children and youth with disabilities have an opportunity to reach their fullest potential.

Best Camps

Best for Baby

Best Camps

The idea of a formal camp experience is, like jazz, an American original. It existed nowhere else, apparently, until Frederick William Gunn, founder of the exclusive Gunnery School in Washington, Connecticut, marched some of his school charges 40 miles south to Long Island Sound during the summer of 1861. They camped "just like soldiers in the Union and Confederate Armies," and news from the battlefronts played a singular part in fueling the imagination of nightly fireside stories. During the day, however, instead of playing soldiers, the young campers played games. Their activites were rounded out by fishing, hiking, and swimming; everyone had such a great time, the idea stuck—and spread. Within a few years, other camps started popping up like mushrooms in damp earth.

In the early days, camping concentrated itself in the Northeast. Attended primarily by boys from affluent families, the camps universally promoted athletics and outdoor activities as a means of developing self-reliance.

Camping did not remain the preserve of the rich for very long, however. Social service agencies identified the benefits of a camp experience for the inner-city poor and began to establish camps for the children of immigrants who were entering the country in waves. The oldest continuing camp, Camp Dudley, was such a camp. It was founded in 1885 by the YMCA and currently is in Westport, New York.

As other parts of the country became more densely populated, camps sprang up nearby. Today there are over 11,000 camps located in all fifty states, and many more in foreign countries as well. Over 4 million children attend camps annually and current estimates list camps as involving over $2 billion dollars of our nation's economy. Although camping today usually embodies the original ideas of its founder— outdoor living, lots of athletic activity, and an emphasis on individual reliance—more and more camps offer special programs concentrating particularly in one skill like oceanography, music, or computers.

The American Camping Association

The American Camping Association, founded in 1910, is a *voluntary* professional organization that provides an accreditation program for camps. It is the oldest accrediting body and the only national one for all types of camps. It currently gives its approval stamp to over 2000 camps nationwide. The ACA seal indicates that the camp meets standards of site, health care, programs provided, personnel, and administration. They recommend the following staff-to-camper ratios:

Age 6 and under: One counselor to five campers
Age 7–8: One counselor to six campers
Age 9–14: One counselor to eight campers
Age 15 and up: One counselor to ten campers

They also recommend that 80% of the staff be 18 or older, and that 20% of staff hold a bachelor's degree. According to their standards, camp directors should hold bachelor's degrees, have a minimum of sixteen previous weeks of administrative experience, and have completed some in-service training in the last three years. Camps are visited in session once every three years to update accreditation.

Some camps that are not ACA members meet these criteria. Some excellent camps do not meet all of them. The ACA sticker simply guarantees certain qualities and its absence does not denote a bad camp. Whether the camp(s) you're considering are accredited or not, *Best For Baby* recommends a thorough investigation of the program, personnel, and history of any camp before enrolling your child.

How to Find a Camp

Newspaper and Magazine Advertising and Guides. The *New York Times* carries the largest advertising section of camps; it appears right after the Christmas season. It is located in the magazine section. *Family Circle* publishes a special *Schools & Camps* section. *Good Housekeeping* also publishes a *Guide to Recommended Schools & Camps*.

Referral Services. Camps usually pay to be listed or represented by these organizations. There's nothing wrong with that, but they obviously push the camps they represent, and you may have to go to more than one to find what you're looking for. Vincent-Curtis in Boston has been around for some time and you can call them at (617) 536-0100 for information.

Camp Fairs. These fairs are held in late winter in many large cities. They can be sponsored by the ACA, a referral service, or a local civic group. Usually they include between 20 and 100 camp representatives who show slides and video tapes, and provide information. Check your local papers around January for notices.

Select-a-Camp. This service is provided by the ACA and is unique in that they will develop a list of ten or more camps from *your criteria* from among the accredited members. Dial 1-800-428-CAMP.

Recommendations from Other Parents. This may be your best bet but begin asking around early. The best camps fill up well ahead of time. If you're lucky, you'll stumble across a camp that doesn't advertise, attend fairs, or use referral services because it's so good it doesn't have to.

The following is a list of camps we like from around the country. ACA camps have an asterisk. Prices are for the summer of 1988 and are approximate.

Alaska Teen Tours
Founded 1980
Eagle River, AK 99577
86 campers, co-ed 15–18,
4 weeks/$3500

A month-long trip through Alaska including visits to the Arctic coast, an Eskimo village, Columbier Glacier, and husky dog teams. Campers also fish, hike, raft, and participate in a wilderness survival camp.

Santa Catalina Summer School Marine Biology Program
Founded 1953
Santa Catalina School,
Monterey, CA 93940*
24 campers, co-ed 10–12, 6 weeks—boarding/$1300; day/$700

Four weeks in Monterey followed by two weeks in Hawaii. Exploration of sea life along the Monterey Pennisula, followed by the reefs of Oahu. (There's a separate camp for girls too.)

Colvig Silver Camps*
Founded 1969
Durango, CO 81301
Co-ed 8–10, girls 11–13, boys 11–13, co-ed 14–18,
4 weeks/$1435, 5 weeks/$1710,
9 weeks/$3000

Campers live in cabins, tents, or teepees. Emphasis on outdoor living and skills in a noncompetitive environment. Expedition trips, rafting, horse packing, backpacking, and rock climbing.

Seacamp*
Founded 1966
Rt. 3, Box 170, Big Pine Key, FL 33043
Co-ed 12–17, 2½ weeks/$1410 (plus $275 for scuba course)

Located at Newfound Harbor on Big Pine Key near the only living coral reef in the United States. Campers live in dorms and cabins and study marine science, campcraft, seamanship, canoeing, lifesaving, arts and crafts, sailing, windsurfing, boating, and scuba.

Midwest Computer Camp*
Founded 1982
9392 Lafayette Road,
Indianapolis, IN 46278
104 campers, co-ed 8–18,
1 week/$400; 2 weeks/$750; 3 weeks/$1100; 4 weeks/$1450.

Dorms, lodge, 50 acres of woods, meadows, and wildlife preserve. All traditional camping activities plus six hours daily on any major brand of computer, all languages. Computer studies can also include work with lasers, robotics, assembly language, and graphics.

Midway-Longview Riding Camp*
Founded 1960
Midway, KY 40347
120 campers, co-ed 5–17, 1–2 weeks/$135–$430

Horsmanship is the main activity with ring instruction, trail rides, and jumping. Swimming, cycling, and dramatics are also available. Campers live in dorms.

**Maine Waterways and
Deer Isle Sailing Center***
Deer Isle, ME
Mailing address: Box 84,
Key Colony Beach, FL 33051
Co-ed 10–18, 2, 3, and 4 week
programs/$595–1170.

Adventurous trip-oriented programs for small groups; sailing, biking,
hiking, and canoeing with expert
guides. Special biking program to Nova
Scotia and along the Maine coast.

Milbrook Sports Camp
Founded 1938
P.O. Box 865, Marshfield, MA 02050
100 boys, 85 girls, 7–16, 8 weeks/
$1950.

Every camper is on a team.
Boston Celtics and Red Sox members
conduct clinics. Basketball, soccer,
tennis, gymnastics, baseball, figure
skating, swimming, sailing, golf,
volleyball, archery, deep sea fishing,
summer stock theater, music, dramatics, and crafts are offered. Whew!

National Music Camp*
Founded 1928
Interlochen, MI 49643
1900 campers, co-ed 8–18, 8 weeks/
$2195

Individual study of the arts, music,
dance, and drama. Private lessons at
additional fees available in all orchestra
instruments, piano, organ, voice, and
classical guitar. There's also a recrea-
tional program in land and water
sports.

**New England Hockey and Figure
Skating Camp***
Founded 1971
Contoocook, NH 03229
60 boys and 60 girls 8–16, 1 week/
$325; 2 weeks/$800; 4 weeks/$1600.
Hockey and figure skating plus land
and water sports.

YMCA Camp Ockanicson*
Founded 1906
Stokes Road,
Box 218, Medford, NJ 08055
Boys 7–16, girls 7–16, co-ed 10–15;
2 weeks/$320 to $430.

Campers live in cabins and dorms.
Specialties include bike trips, trip
camping, tennis, ranching, leadership
training, western and English riding,
video making, computers, and BMX
bikes.

Brush Ranch Camps*
Founded 1957
Tererro, NM 87573
50 boys 8–14, 70 girls 8–17, separate
camps. 4 weeks/$1150; 8 weeks/$2200

Located on the Pecos River with
289 private acres at an elevation of
7600 feet and surrounded by the Santa
Fe National Forest. Cabins. Girls:
horses, swimming, tennis, art, dance,
drama, music, nature studies and pack
trips by horseback. Boys: tennis,
riflery, skeet shooting, swimming,
fencing, back packing, arts and crafts,
nature, drama, and ropes courses.

Camp Winding Gap*
Rt. 1, Box 56,
Lake Toxaway, NC 28747
Co-ed 8–15, 2, 3, 5 weeks and
longer/$300 per week

Traditional Appalachian farm
nestled amid thousands of acres of
unspoiled natural beauty. Western
riding with overnight camp outs,
whitewater rafting, canoeing, tubing,
archery, riflery, rock climbing, backpacking, photography, nature study,
music, clogging, arts and crafts,
woodworking, hands-on experience
with farm animals, including llamas,
cooking and sewing.

Camp Ballibay*
Founded 1960
Box 1, Camptown, PA 18815
55 campers, co-ed 6–16, 2 weeks/
$625; 3 weeks/$975; 4 weeks/$1375;
7 weeks/$2175

Cabins, hundreds of acres in the
Allegheny mountains, noncompetitive
and structured for individual choice,
beautiful theater. Classes in mime,
magic, voice, TV, dance, chamber
music, orchestra, vocal and instru-
mental music. Fine arts studies in
printmaking, ceramics, jewelry. Also
riding and sports.

Ghost Canyon Ranch
Founded 1967
Hermosa, SD 57744
20 campers, boys 9–13, girls 10–17,
2 weeks/$450.

Ranch camp in the Black Hills,
riding, overnight camping, sports,
swimming, hootenannies. Each camper
is assigned his or her own horse and is
responsible for its well-being.

Camp Stewart for Boys*
Founded 1924
Hunt, TX 78024
Boys 6–14, 34 day sessions/$1100

Oldest continually operating camp
in the Southwest. Over 500 acres on
headwaters of the Guadelupe River in
Texas hill country. Each summer 80%
of the campers return. Emphasis is on
personal growth. Swimming, canoeing,
sailing, water skiing, western and English equitation (over 100 camp-owned
horses), football, baseball, track,
soccer, gymnasium for basketball and
wrestling, seven tennis courts, NRA
riflery, CAA archery, campcraft, nature
and ecology, crafts and music.

Kiniya*
Founded 1919
Milton, VT 05468
Girls 6–17, 4 weeks/$1600,
8 weeks/$2650

Cabins and lodge. Traditional New
England camp in a lovely setting over-
looking Lake Champlain. Riding, sailing, tennis, waterskiing, gymnastics,
crafts, dance, drama, hiking trips. Special program in Ireland for three weeks
for older girls.

Legacy International Youth Program*
Founded 1976
Rt. 4, Box 265, Bedford, VA 24523
120 campers, co-ed 9–18,
6 weeks/$1650

Located in the foothills of the
Blue Ridge Mountains. Emphasizes
international understanding. Campers
come from many ethnic, national, and
racial backgrounds. Water sports,
hiking and camping, language studies,
computers, theater, arts and crafts.

Canoe Island Camps, Institut Francile*
Founded 1969
P.O. Box 185, Eastsound, WA 98245
30 campers, co-ed 10–15, 2 weeks/
$700; 3 weeks/$1012; 4 weeks/$1325;
5 weeks/$1725

Cabins and teepees. Located in the San Juan Islands in Puget Sound. Learn the French language and French traditions while enjoying water and land sports, theater, and crafts. Overnight trips to other San Juan Islands.

Camp Fiesta*
Founded 1938
P.O. Box 317,
Boulder Junction, WI 54512
90 campers, girls 8–16, 3½ weeks/
$1000.

Cabins snuggled against the edge of a 4000-acre lake. Scuba and equitation along with basic horse care. Three hours of riding daily.

Elk Creek Ranch*
Sunlight Valley, Wyoming
mailing address:
P.O. Box 1476,
Cody, WY 82414
Co-ed 30-day ranch program, ages
13–17/$1500
Co-ed 30-day range trek program, ages
15–18/$1400

Owned by the same family for thirty years. Located in a valley at an elevation of 6000 feet with mountains ranging to 13,000 feet. Many options in the ranch program. Treks go to Absaroka and Beartooth wilderness areas, one focusing on mountain ascents and the other on fishing.

Specialty Camps

United States Space Camp
Founded 1982
The Space and Rocket Center,
Tranquility Base, Huntsville, AL 35807
Co-ed 11–16, $350–$400 per week

Focus on astronaut training, simulated space shuttle missions, and space-lab experience. Campers participate in demonstrations at the Alabama Space and Rocket Center Mission and visit labs at NASA Marshall Space Flight Center.

Mystic Mariner Programs*
Founded 1949
Mystic Seaport Museum, Inc.
Mystic, CT 06355
55 campers, co-ed 12–17, $210/week

Campers live aboard the Joseph Conrad for a week. Sailing, seamanship, and maritime history. Also fishing, shipbuilding, sea chanteys, nineteenth-century life, tools, and crafts.

Culver Summer Camps*
Founded 1902
Culver Academies, Box 138,
Culver, IN 46511
220 campers, co-ed 9–17,
13 days/$600, 7 weeks/$1750

All normal camping activities plus fifteen specialty flying camps, including a flight training center, ground and flight training. Twelve hours of flight instruction leading to solo and FAA certification.

Camp Marchand
701 East Bay, Suite 3-203,
Charleston, SC 29403
35 campers, co-ed 10–16,
4 weeks/$1200

Located in the farming village of Mosac in southwest France, this camp acquaints its attendees with language, culture, and local French people. It is housed in a historic sixteenth-century French farm. Campers participate in daily classes of French, cooking, drama, nature, weaving, hiking and sports. A two-day trip to Paris is included.

Special Campers

Sherwood Forest *
Founded 1936
Lesterville, MO 63654
100 campers, boys 10–16, girls 10–16, co-ed 7–13
Fees based on ability to pay.
Offers 487 acres of forests and lakes, crafts, hiking, canoeing, and experiential growth. Special handicap program for ages 8–13 with minor disabilities who are able to interact with normal children.

Spring Creek Mountain/Desert Survival School
Founded 1979
Spring Creek Community, P.O. Box 429, Thompson Falls, MT 58873
Co-ed 13–18

A 3–week survival trip and year-round wilderness school designed for youths who may be involved in substance abuse or have special educational or emotional needs. Through group pressure as well as solitude, students are taught to take a good look ‹ at themselves, their behavior, and their priorities. Supplementary activities include rock climbing, mountaineering, kayaking, rafting, and mountain rescue.

Glyndon Camp for Diabetic Children
Founded 1960
407 Central Avenue, Reistertown, MD 21136
200 campers, co-ed 5–17 1 week/ $195, 2 weeks/$390

For diabetics and operated by the Maryland Diabetes Association. Nature study, swimming, sports trips, arts and crafts, cookouts. Campers learn to manage their disease by diet, exercise, and insulin management.

Best Athletic Equipment

Best Athletic Equipment

If you are under the impression that children naturally stay fit because of their inherent youthful energy or muscle tone, consider these statistics. Children today are fatter than they were in the 1960s and watch an average of six hours of TV per day. (An entirely unrelated study purports to show that a human burns fewer calories lying on a couch and watching TV than just lying on a couch!) A recent report by the Presidential Council on Fitness based on a study of 18,000 children nationwide concludes that indeed the youth of this country are in terrible shape. One in four boys aged 6 to 12 could not do *a single pull-up*. Yet another study by researchers at the University of Michigan showed that 40% of the first through third graders they studied had at least one risk factor for heart disease!

Your child's fitness is in your hands. Researchers of the exercise habits of the young have discovered that fourth grade seems to be the magic age. By that time, attitudes toward exercise seem fixed. These researchers caution against going overboard in encouraging athletics. "Exercise" as a concept has no meaning for children. They have to be having fun. Setting an example yourself and limiting TV will do the trick.

When purchasing athletic equipment for children, try to find products designed for your child's weight, height, and motor abilities. Don't stint. Poor equipment that's too large or difficult to manipulate can discourage even the most enthusiastic budding athlete.

What follows is a selection of fine equipment for a number of disciplines. Remember you do not need to outfit your child with a slew of expensive paraphernalia to guarantee a decent heart rate. A ball and a jump rope are a great way to begin. All items listed are suitable for both sexes unless specified otherwise.

Best for Baby

Spaulding Skill Builders Series

This line of balls for soccer, basketball, and football is designed especially to develop the skills of young athletes. These balls are made from the same high quality materials as the full-size products. Their size and construction give a child more control over the ball and added confidence to maximize his or her own ability. *$12.99 for 2 balls, $7.99 each.* Spaulding also makes a 28½ inch circumference basketball for women and youth for *$29.99*

Baseball

The Cooper Company

The Black Diamond is the most popular junior glove made by Cooper for boys or girls with small hands. It has a deep pocket, double bar strap trap, firm thumb, and is well-padded with strong lightweight felt. *This 10½-inch tanned leather glove retails for $24. The Black Diamond Little League catcher's mitt is $36.*

Black Diamond Tournament Little League Aluminum Bat

This bat is available in a 28-inch length, perfect for small hitters. It features an extra large, 2¼-inch diameter barrel. *$34.*

Professional Little League Wooden Bat

This bat is made from the highest-quality second growth white ash. It is flame-treated and has a thin handle for small hands. Available in 28-inch lengths and up. *$13. Note:* Cooper has a range of helmets, masks, and protective gear as well for the young player.

Nerf Softball

The Parker Company makes this ball, and it is suitable for ages 5 and up. The **Nerf** is bright yellow for high visibility. The foam construction makes it softer and safer than a regular softball, but the power core and the tough durable cover let it be thrown, caught, and hit like one. They make a volleyball of the same materials. *Softball: $6.95, volleyball: $16.45.*

Hockey

The Cooper Company

The Cooper Company (see baseball) is also known for its high-quality hockey equipment. They make two different beginner skates in sizes 10 to 13 (full sizes only). The Cooper Y50 has nylon quarters, toe, and tongue. The skates are leather-lined and have leather trim and uppers. A tough premolded plastic toe and padded ankles protect young feet. *Retail: $67.50.* The Y60 is identical except for nylon trim and split leather lining. *Retail: $53.00.* Cooper also makes a skate for more advanced young skaters called the Cooper Custom Pro Junior. It is hand-lasted and has all the features of an adult pro-quality skate. *Retail: $161.*

Hockey Sticks

The Cooper Laser/Tyke hockey stick has a two-piece selected hardwood handle and blade. It is 45 inches long and ideal for players age 4 to 7. *Retail: $6.30.* For older players they have well-made and designed sticks in 46- and 49-inch lengths *ranging in price from $8.90 to $16.50.* Cooper also makes helmets, masks, and protective gear for youngsters and produces a special line for girls.

Swimming

Aqua Learn

One of the cleverest swimming aids we've ever seen is this suit with built-in flotation pieces by this California company. The suit puts your child in a naturally balanced swimming position—upright and tilted slightly forward. As your child becomes more confident in water, you can gradually remove the styrofoam pieces. Recommended by swimming instructors. Available in red, blue, or yellow for ages 18 months and up. *Approximate retail: $22.*

Best for Baby

Fishing

The Orvis company based in Manchester, Vermont is one of the world's leading makers of fishing equipment. For fledgling fishermen they recommend the Far and Fine/ Green Mountain Series. The 7-foot 9-inch graphite rod may still be a bit heavy for beginners but the rod is very durable and can be used for a lifetime. The package also comes with rod, reel, line, leader, backing, case, and introductory booklet. *Retail: $149.50.*

Bicycles

Peugeot Tricycles

These small three-wheeled bikes have European styling and the same high production standards as any **Peugeot** product. Available in pink and aqua. *Retail: $44.95.*

Skiing

Dynastar Bora

Unlike many companies, Dynastar actually designs their kids' skis to childsize proportions. The **Bora** has a polyurethane-injected foam core for flexibility, the key feature of a quality child's ski. *Retail: $95*. For boots, we like Salomon's SX 11 Mini. This is a rear-entry boot, like all Salomans, and much easier to put on than traditional models. It is made from especially flexible plastic for easy forward flex. A free-floating cuff makes the mini more comfortable for playing in the lodge too. Best of all there's just one buckle! *Approximate retail: $85*. Saloman also makes an ultra-lightweight child's binding, the S127 Mini. *Approximate retail: $60*.

Tennis

Prince J/R Star

This is the perfect racket for the 3- to 5-year-old future tennis star. It's just 21 inches long, with an extra small grip, but it still has that famous outsized **Prince** head for easier hitting. *Retail: $21.50*

Prince J/R Tour

Two inches longer than its predecssor, this is the racket of choice for 5 to 7 years olds. Eighty-five square inches of head surface help make those tough cross-court shots. *Retail: $26.50*.

Allergies & Orthodontia

Best for Baby

Allergies & Orthodontia

Allergies

Allergies, quite simply, are a reaction of the immune system to certain proteins that are otherwise harmless. For a universal threat like a virus, we all produce antibodies. In an allergic reaction, a person produces an excess of a specific group of antibodies called IgE to the allergen, or allergy-causing substance. Some common allergens are animal dander, ragweed pollen, and dust. Two common and extremely dangerous allergens are penicillin and insect stings. (Penicillin allergies can be so deadly that once an allergy is suspected, most doctors won't even test for it because even in infinitesmal amounts it has proved life-threatening!) You can do little to prevent allergies, for they are strongly hereditary. One thing that does help prevent _food_ allergies is breastfeeding. Breast milk contains certain IgA immunoglobins that are deficient in the systems of very young babies. Studies show that these immunoglobins protect the intestinal lining from adverse reactions to various food proteins until a baby's digestion can handle them.

To identify allergies in infants is a difficult job unless their allergy is unusually severe. Many allergies are seasonal or occasional, and the vast range of allergic symptoms often leads parents to confuse allergies with other illnesses. If you suspect your infant or toddler of developing allergies, pay attention to when, where, and what type of reaction occurs. The first step in diagnosis is a careful personal history and a physical exam.

Allergy therapy generally occurs in three forms. **Pills** or **inhalants** are frequently used for seasonal allergens like ragweed. They are also used to treat occasional allergens like allergy-causing foods that are accidentally consumed. Peanut product and egg white allergies are often treated this way.

For more serious and continual allergic reactions (to dust, for example), many opt for **allergy shots**. Shots are expensive, however, and don't cure anything. They just cover symptoms.

A third method that works well for certain kinds of allergies is **Desensitization**. Miniscule but increasing doses of an allergen are administered over time to build immune-system tolerance to the substance. Instead of IgE, the body begins to produce IgG antibodies that combine with the allergen to block the release of histamines, the substances that cause symptoms. Desensitization is not unrelated to homeopathic remedies described below.

For more information on children and allergies, try the following:

Parents' Book of Childhood Allergies by Richard F. Graber, Ballantine Books/Random House, $2.95.

Allergies and the Hyperactive Child by Doris J. Rapp, M.D., Simon and Schuster, $7.95.

Two Alternative Allergy Treatments

Acupuncture

Acupuncture is the oldest system of medicine still in practice. Records of acupuncture treatment go back over 5000 years. According to this medical philosophy, an energy called *ch'i* flows throughout the universe and all persons. An internal interruption of the ch'i is essentially what creates a disease, or in the topic we're talking about, an allergic reaction. By inserting needles an eighth to a quarter of an inch deep into certain points along ch'i pathways, or energy meridians as others call them, an acupuncturist can stimulate the ch'i and restore internal balance and health. Different illnesses require different points of treatment. Doctors may choose from over 800! All acupuncturists are quick to point out, however, that they treat the whole person, not just a symptom or disease.

A good acupuncturist will be the first to tell you that this form of medicine may be less appropriate than a western approach for certain diseases. But less acute forms of allergies often clear up considerably when treated by acupuncture. Unlike many Western approaches, the aim is to cure the allergy entirely, not merely eliminate the symptoms. This process can take several months of weekly visits, but it is certainly better than a lifetime of shots!

Skillfully applied, the needles are painless. If you are interested in treating a younger child, often it helps if he sees a parent undergo a treatment first. Because proper diagnosis is based on a lengthy patient history with lots of questions about cravings, moods, etc., some acupuncturists prefer not to treat infants. If you choose to try acupuncture, do consult with, or at least inform, your regular doctor about the treatments, as well.

The National Commission for Certification of Acupuncturists in conjunction with traditional medical doctors has formulated a certification program for practicing acupuncturists. It involves a day-long exam, proof of apprenticeship, and a three-year degree requirement with a minimum GPA. For a referral to a certified acupuncturist in your area, you may write to the commission at:

NCAA
1424 16th Street, NW
Washington, D.C. 20036

Homeopathy

Homeopathy, in contrast to acupuncture, was discovered only 200 years ago by Samuel Hahnemann, a German physician. Its basic principle is to activate and strengthen a weak or malfunctioning immune system; it is extremely effective in treating allergies.

In Europe, it has achieved widespread acceptance. The British royal family swear by it, with the Queen heading the list.

Like most M.D.s, homeopaths believe that symptoms are adaptations of our bodies to stress and disease. In the case of allergies, they would say that the stress is too strong for the body to heal alone, and that it needs an outside catalyst to boost the healing process. They prescribe from a range of homeopathic medicines derived from over 2000 entirely natural plant, animal, and mineral sources. Prescription is based on a "like cures like" theory. A practitioner seeks to find a substance that in sufficient doses will make a healthy person ill with the same symptoms a sick person has now. Each patient case is regarded as completely unique and medicines are prescribed according to the totality of symptoms—there are no routine prescriptions. The process of discovering the exact substance that will cure a given individual is the art of this medical science.

Many homeopaths in this country are also licensed M.D.s. To obtain a referral for a homeopath in your area, write or call:

The National Center for
Homeopathy
1500 Massachusetts
Avenue, N.W. Suite 41
Washington, D.C. 20005
(202) 223-6182

Orthodontia

As you begin to care for your new baby, orthodontia may be the furthest thing from your mind. But as you carry your newborn home from the hospital, he already has his first full, if invisible, set of teeth, and his body has gone to work on producing a second. Braces aren't a consideration until permanent teeth make their appearance between the ages of 6 and 12. But more and more evidence points to early attention and care as the best means of preventing the need for extensive treatment later on.

Orthodontic problems are caused by two things: heredity and habit. (In very rare cases they can also be caused by an early childhood accident.) Teeth can be crowded, crooked, or too far apart. There can be an incorrect bite with an upper jaw jutting too far forward or too far back. Straight, evenly spaced teeth are healthier. They don't stick out, reducing chance of damage. They decay less because they're easier to clean. Poor positioning of teeth or bite may even affect a person's speech.

A new wave of dentists specializing in children's teeth (called pedodontists) has recently begun to flourish. They can see children as young as 6 months and recommend the first visit occurring by age 3 at the latest. At that time they will examine bite, tongue, and lip movements that may influence tooth growth, and teach proper care of teeth. A full set of x-rays, once de rigueur, is no longer necessary unless there's an obvious problem.

They *will* take a set of x-rays if they feel braces or any other corrective measures are necessary. Sometimes a palatal expander to widen the jaw, or a removable retainer to correct the position of a few key teeth, is all your child will need if his problem is detected early enough. If your dentist or pedodontist does recommend a full set of braces, there's a fine new option available: invisible braces of man-made sapphire. The impurities that give natural sapphires their color aren't present. Brackets are still connected with metal wire, but work on creating near-invisible wire is going on. By the time your infant is ready

Care of Infant Teeth

The ADA recommends that you:

• Take your child to the dentist by age 2.
• Put only water in your child's bottle during naps and at night to prevent the serious decay called "nursing bottle mouth."
• Start cleaning your child's teeth daily as soon as the first tooth appears. (The Mag Mag Ortho Training System in the Feeding Gear section is an excellent training device, and a help during teething too.)
• Ask your dentist for directions in brushing and flossing teeth. Although your child may want to brush by himself, you should probably oversee flossing. (Some dentists feel that flossing is unnecessary until a child can do it alone, around age 8).
• Make sure your child is getting enough (but not too much) flouride. Nursing mothers may especially want to add a few drops to their baby's diet. Although nursing strengthens jaw muscles and is credited with aiding in the growth of straigther teeth, human milk contains only trace amounts of this vital mineral.

Best for Baby

• If a tooth is knocked out . . .

Rinse the tooth in cool water and try to put it back in its socket for at least 5 minutes. If this isn't possible, place the tooth in a cup of water or milk, or wrap it in a wet cloth. Whatever you do, don't scrub the tooth! Head immediately to the nearest dentist—time is of the essence. In many cases, teeth that are put back in the mouth within a half hour will heal and function normally with no further attention.

for braces, this invisible wire may be available. The new braces cost about 10% more than the old metal variety, but many parents feel that it's worth it, especially in cases where the child is particularly self-conscious.

If you need an orthodontist, your dentist will usually have one they like to work with. But getting on with your own dentist doesn't necessarily mean getting on with the referred orthodontist, and it's a relationship where good communication is crucial. Good idea to shop around and compare fees where so much money ($2500 to $3500 on average) may be at stake. If your own dentist cannot recommend an orthodonist, the ADA will refer members in your area. You can write them at:

American Dental Association
211 East Chicago Avenue
Chicago, IL 60611

Note: They also provide free information on orthodontia and other tooth problems for the asking.

Shopping Guide

Best for Baby

Shopping Guide

Note: When calling a manufacturer or distributor for information, ask for the customer
service department unless
otherwise specified. Mail order
on a product is available *only*
when specified.

Cribs

Zenith
Lewis of London stores are
located in the following cities:
Woodbury, Forest Hills, Man-
hasset, White Plains and New
York, New York; Paramus,
Mountain and Englishtown, NJ;
Rockville, MD; Newton Centre,
MA; Wynnewood and Hunting-
ton Valley, PA; St. Louis, MO;
Atlanta, GA; Highland Park, IL;
La Jolla, CA; and Falls Church,
VA.

Rimini
Available mainly in higher-end
baby specialty stores. Also
from Baby's Room, Baby Toy-
town, and Bergstrom's. For
further information contact:

Tracers
612 Waverly Avenue
Mamaroneck, New York 10543
(914) 381-5777

Crib 'n Bed
Childcraft is a widely distributed line in baby specialty
stores, baby discount outlets,
and regular furniture outlets.
For the name of a dealer near
you contact:

Childcraft
P.O. Box 444
Salem, Indiana 47167
(812) 883-3111

Granada
This crib is new to the market
and carried only in baby specialty shops. For information
contact:

Marshall Baby Care Products
600 Barclay Blvd.
Lincolnshire, IL 60069
(800) 634-4350

Country Crib
Fisher-Price products are distributed widely in toy outlets,
discount merchandisers,
department stores and children's specialty shops. Their
line is so readily available that
they offer no customer referrals and suggest calling stores
in your area.

Palermo
Simmons cribs are distributed
by over 800 dealers nationally.
If you are unable to locate the
dealer nearest you contact:

Simmons Juvenile Products
Company, Inc.
613 East Beacon Avenue
New London, Wisconsin
54961
(412) 982-2140

Travel Cot
Baby Björn is available at
Nordstrom's, Marshall Field's,
Bloomingdale's, and FAO
Schwartz. If they do not carry
a particular item, they can
order it for you. The line is
also widely available at baby
specialty boutiques. Or contact:

Baby Björn
P.O. Box 1322
Shaker Heights, Ohio 44120
(216) 662-2922

Sam's Crib
Contact the woodworker
directly:

Dan Moshein
P.O. Box 2660
Red Mountain Road
Arlington, VT 05250
(802) 375-2568

Evelyn
See Zenith crib information.

Commuter
The Newborne line is carried
in many baby specialty shops
as well as Childworld. If you
cannot find the crib in one of
these places, contact:

The Newborne Company
River Road
Worthington, MA 01098
(413) 238-5551

Lamby
Widely available through juvenile specialty stores, or contact:

Lamby
3820 Bodega Avenue
P.O. Box 5125
Petaluma, CA 94953
(707) 763-4222

Mattresses

Sealy Posturepedic Mattress
This line is distributed by
Gerry Baby Products. For the
store nearest you contact:

Gerry Baby Products
12520 Grant Drive
Denver, CO 80233
(303) 457-0926

Firm 150 Heavy Duty Coil Design
This mattress is from Okla
Homer Smith, one of the
family of companies owned by
the Gerber Furniture Group.
Various parts of the entire line
are carried by Sears, Penneys,
Childworld, and Toys R Us. To
find out where this and other
products are sold in your area,
contact:

Consumer Service Department
Gerber Furniture Group, Inc.
9600 Valley View Road
Macedonia, OH 44056
(800) 222-9825
In Ohio (800) 686-2229

Baby Beautyrest
See Palermo under Cribs.

Flotation Crib Mattress
This mattress can be purchased
directly from the manufacturer. Contact:

California Concepts
2234 Gladwick
Compton, CA 90220
(213) 537-0161

Crib Futon
Contact:

Burlington Futon Company
388 Pine Street
Burlington, VT 05401
(802) 862-5056

Playpens and Infant Seats

Thru-the-Door
For the store nearest you contact:

Kolcraft Products
5133 West 66th Street
Bedford Park, IL 60638
(800) 453-7673

40 Inch Activity Playard
This is from Century, a division of Gerber. Their products
are widely carried nationwide.
For information on where a
specific product is available
nearest you, contact:

Consumer Service Department
Gerber Furniture Group, Inc.
9600 Valley View Road
Macedonia, Ohio 44056
(800) 222-9825
In Ohio (800) 686-2229

Travel Tender
See Fisher-Price information
under Country Crib in Cribs.

Best for Baby

Folding 40 Deluxe Play Yard

See Sealy Posturepedic under Mattresses for information.

Century Crawlspace

See 40 Inch Activity Playard for information.

Wooden Playpen

Available through the Rifton Community Catalog. For a free copy contact:

Community Playthings
Route 213
Rifton, New York 12471
(914) 658-3141

Great Kid's Porta-Pad

For the store nearest you contact:

The Great Kid Company
P.O. Box 654
Lexington, MA 02173
(617) 254-0859

Bouncer Infant Carrier

The Snugli line is widely available in baby specialty stores. Sears has also carried their products. For a Snugli dealer near you contact:

Snugli
12980 West Cedar Drive
Lakewood, CO 80228
(303) 457-0926

Tyke-Hike Baby Rocker

This company's line is carried by Marshall Field's, Thalhimer's, and better baby specialty stores. For more information contact:

Tyke Corporation
1165 N. Clark Street
Suite 400
Chicago, IL 60610
(800) 533-8953

Summer Comfort Seat System IV

This and other Summer products are carried in better baby specialty shops. For the store nearest you contact:

Summer Infant Products, Inc.
711 Branch Avenue
Providence, RI 02904
(401) 421-1360

Johnny Jump-up Gym Seat

This and other Evenflo products are carried by Sears, Toys R Us, and many baby specialty stores. For specific information for a store in your area contact:

Evenflo
1801 Commerce Drive
Piqua, Ohio 45356
(800) 233-5921
In Ohio (800) 233-5920

Carriages and Strollers

Ringo

The Emmaljunga line is carried by Neiman-Marcus, Nordstrom's, Saks Fifth Avenue and better baby stores. To locate a store near you, contact:

Bandaks Emmaljunga, Inc.
7880 Convoy Court
San Diego, CA 92111
(619) 576-9990

911s

This is a new model for On the Town and is just coming into the stores. For a store location near you contact:

On the Town
601 16th Street
Carlstadt, NJ 07072
(201) 939-4300

Blue Candy Stripe

See Thru-the-Door under Playpens for Kolcraft information.

Quattro Domani

This stroller is carried by Toys R Us and baby specialty shops. For the store nearest you, contact:

Peg Perego U.S.A. Inc.
3625 Independent Drive
Fort Wayne, IN 46818
(219) 484-2940

Silver Shadow Esprit

For information on the store nearest you, contact:

Patty Tripp
Alcot Industries, Inc.
361 Alden Road
Markham, Ontario L3R 3L4, Canada
(416) 474-0101

Maclaren Dreamer

The Dreamer is carried in better baby stores. For the location nearest you, contact:

Marshall Baby Care Products
600 Barclay Blvd.
Lincolnshire, IL 60069
(800) 634-4350

Jane/Janette

See information on Maclaren Dreamer in this section.

Double Fold 'n Go

This is a Century product from the Gerber group. See 40 Inch Activity Playard in the Playpens section for shopping information.

Car Seats

Fisher-Price Car Seat

See Country Crib under Cribs section for Fisher-Price shopping information.

Special Touring Edition 2000

See 40 Inch Activity Playard for Century shopping information.

Ultra Ride

See Thru-the-Door under Playpens for Kolcraft shopping information.

Seven Year Carseat

See Evenflo shopping information under Johnny Jump-up Gym Seat in the Playpens and Infant Seats section.

Guardian 653

The Gerry line is carried by many major chains including Walmart's, Sears, Penney's, Toys 'R Us, and Childworld. For information on the store nearest you that carries a particular product, contact:

Gerry Baby Products
12520 Grant Drive
Denver, CO 80233
(303) 457-0926

GT 2000

For Strolee shopping information, contact:

Strolee
P.O. Box 5786
10967 South Reyes
Rancho Dominguez, CA 90244
(213) 639-9300

Swings

Port-A-Swing

See Fisher-Price shopping information under Country Crib in Cribs section.

Sing 'n Swing

See Strolee shopping information under the GT 2000 in the Car Seat section.

Evenflo Swing/Carseat/Carrier

This product is relatively new to the marketplace. For Evenflo shopping information, see the Johnny Jump-up Gym Seat under the Playpens and Infant Seats section.

Easy Entry Swyngomatic

Graco is a widely distributed line of products. For the store nearest you contact:

Graco Children's Products, Inc.
Elverson, PA 19520
(215) 286-5951

Sound Starter with Kanga Rocka Roo

This is a Century product. Please see shopping information under 40 Inch Activity Playard in Playpens section.

Best for Baby

Carriers

Snugli Original

The Snugli line of carriers is widely available in baby stores. For the store nearest you, see shopping information under the Bouncer Infant Carrier in the Playpens and Infant Seats section.

The Safe Baby Carrier

See shopping information on Baby Björn products under Travel Cot in the Cribs section.

Snugli Soft Infant Carrier

See shopping information under Bouncer Infant Carrier in Playpens and Infant Seats section.

Sara's Ride

This carrier is available through Children's World, baby specialty stores, or directly from the manufacturer. Send a check or money order for $24.95 to:

Sara's Ride, Inc.
2448 Blake Street
Denver, CO 80205
(303) 292-2224

Woven Palm Leaf Carrier

This is carried in better baby specialty stores including Bellini, Lewis of London, Bergstrom's and Baby Toy Town among others. For information on the store nearest you contact:

Kids Corp. International
12020 S.W. 114th Place
Miami, FL 33176
(305) 255-0014

Colt

Tough Traveler products are available through L.L. Bean, REI, and many backpack and mountaineering shops. For the store nearest you contact:

Tough Traveler
1012 State Street
Schenectady, NY 12307
(518) 377-8526

Carta-Kid

See Great Kid Co. shopping information under Porta-Pad in the Playpens section.

Cozy Toes Carry Cot

See Baby Björn shopping information under Travel Cot in Cribs section.

Portable Kiddie Seats

For Gerry product shopping information, see Sealy Posturepedic Mattress under Cribs section.

Cuddlepack

For Gerry shopping information see Guardian 653 under Car Seats.

Diapers

Pampers, Huggies and Luvs are all widely available in grocery and discount outlets. All other products listed in this section can be obtained from at least one of the children's clothing catalogs in the Best Clothing section. For a diaper service near you, check the yellow pages.

Ointments and Lotions

Johnson & Johnson

These products are widely available.

Vaseline Petroleum Jelly

Widely available.

Desitin

Widely available.

Borofax

This is a bit difficult to locate. Try calling 1-800-642-3194 for a store near you.

A & D Ointment

Widely availble.

Weleda

This line is primarily available in health food stores. They also have a mail order service. For a catalog contact:

Weleda Pharmacy, Inc.
841 South Main Street
P.O. Box 769
Spring Valley, NY 10977
(914) 352-6145

Autumn Harp

This line is available primarily through health food stores. They will also respond to mail orders. Contact:

Autumn Harp, Inc.
28 Rockydale Road
Bristol, VT 05443
(802) 453-4807

Mobiles

Elephant Party

This can be ordered through the Museum of Modern Art's catalog, a free copy of which you can receive by calling 1-800-553-5464. In Ohio dial 1-800-282-0746.

Voice-activated Mobile

This mobile is available only through the Johnson & Johnson baby products catalog. Dial 1-800-223-8916 for a free copy.

Clowning Around

This mobile is available from Bergstrom's, Macy's, Filene's, Bellini, and the Right Start Catalog, as well as better baby stores. For information on the store nearest you, contact:

Dakin
P.O. Box 7746
San Francisco, CA 94120
(800) 227-6598

Bright Baby Mobile

This mobile is available exclusively through F.A.O. Schwarz stores and their catalog. For a catalog, send $5.00 to:

F.A.O. Schwarz
1 Yellow Brick Road
Ridgely, MD 21685

Or call 1-800-426-TOYS and charge it to your credit card. With either method of payment, you will receive a $10 gift certificate with your first order.

Toys

Rattle

This rattle is available primarily through independent toy shops and the Hearth Song (see Toy section) and Garnet Hill (see Clothing section) catalogs. For information on the store nearest you, contact:

Elwood Turner
Box HC132
Morrisville, VT 05661
(802) 888-3375

Car Seat Circus

This is a Summer product. See shopping information under Summer Comfort Seat System in Playpens and Infant Seats section.

Tender Teddy

Gund bears are widely distributed in better toy shops.

Bright Baby Tactile Tillie

See F.A.O. Schwarz shopping information under Bright Baby Mobile in the Mobiles section.

Animal Sound Barn

The Fisher-Price toy line is among the most widely distributed in the country. This should be available locally in several places.

Rattle Ball

This ball is available through Waldenkids, Mr. G's and Ricky's Toys as well as many independent toy stores. For information on a store near you, call 1-800-247-6144.

Turtle Sandbox

This item is available through Sears, Penney's, Toys R Us, Childworld, and many independent toy stores. For the name of a store near you call Little Tikes at 1-800-321-0183.

Paddleboat

This is available through some toy stores, the Hearth Song catalog (see catalogs in Best Toys) or directly from the manufacturer. Contact:

The Woodworks Toy
    Company
505 Southeast Vera
Corvallis, OR 97333
(505) 752-0991

Gentle Mouse Bouncer

This is distributed in better baby stores. For the name of a store near you, contact:

First Step Designs, Ltd.
1574 Centre Street
Newton, MA 02161
(617) 527-3043

Original Gloucester Rocker

This is available in better toy stores and a number of marine shops. For the name of a store near you write:

Gloucester Rockers Ltd.
811 Boylston Street
Boston, MA 02116

Block Crayons

These are distributed by Hearth Song. See information under Truth's Baby Doll above.

Truth's Baby Doll

This is available through the Hearth Song catalog. For a free catalog, call (707) 829-1550.

Bright Blocks

These blocks are sold through Penney's, Woolworth's, Toys R Us, and Childworld along with many other stores nationwide.

My Train

This is available through a number of top toy stores or directly from the manufacturer. For a store near you or to order directly contact:

Montgomery Schoolhouse
Montgomery, VT 05470
(802) 326-4272

Wooden Blocks

These are available through the Community Playthings catalog. For a free copy contact:

Community Playthings
Route 213
Rifton, NY 12471
(914) 658-3141

Kindercolor Express

This is available through a number of catalogs and fine toy and baby stores. For information on the store nearest you, contact:

Kinderworks Corporation
P.O. Box 1441
Portsmouth, NH 03801
(603) 436-1441

Omagles

This is a Gerber product. For shopping information see 40 inch Activity Playard under Playpens.

Tyke Hike Toybox

This product is new to the marketplace. For information on a store near you, see shopping information under Tyke Hike Rocker in the Playpens and Infant Seats section.

Playcraft Bookcase with Cubbies

See Tike shopping information under Turtle Sandbox above.

Clothing

Florence Eiseman

The Eiseman line is carried by Neiman-Marcus, Saks Fifth Avenue, Garfinckel's, Marshall Field's, Nordstrom's, and specialty children's shops.

Rothchild and Company

This line is carried by Lord & Taylor's, Macy's, Bloomingdale's, Marshall Field's, Dillard's and better children's clothing stores. For the name of a store near you call (212) 564-2978.

Laura Ashley

This line is available in part from many Laura Ashley stores. They have also opened a number of Laura Ashley Mother & Child stores that specialize in this particular line alone. Check with the Laura Ashley stores nearest you.

John-John Suit

Imp Originals distributes to finer children's clothing and department stores. For more information contact:

Imp Originals
112 West 34th Street
New York, NY 10018

Smocked Dress

Denny Buckley primarily distributes through trunk shows at better department stores. She also does a large mail order business. You can contact her at:

Nantucket Designs
12 Orange Street
Nantucket, MA 02554
(617) 228-2996

All clothing catalog information is in the Best Clothes section itself.

Food & Diet

Baby's Garden

Available in health food stores and some supermarkets.

Earth's Best

Available in health food stores and some supermarkets. For information on a store near you call (802) 388-7974.

Beech-Nut

Widely available nationwide.

Heinz

Widely available nationwide.

Feeding Gear

Ansä

Widely available nationwide.

Nuk

Widely available nationwide.

Nursä

Widely available nationwide.

Púr

Widely available nationwide.

Remond

Available in some baby stores or directly from Handy Chair Corporation, the importer. Call them at (800) 426-9244 or write:

Handy Chair
5742 Lorelei Avenue
Lakewood, CA 90712

Mag Mag Training Cup System

This is available in better baby shops. For more shopping information or stores in your area see the Granada under Cribs.

Ring Around

Available in some drug stores and baby stores. For more information contact:

A-Plus Products, Inc.
P.O. Box 2975
Beverly Hills, CA 90213
(213) 204-2024

Deluxe High Chair

See Gerry shopping information under Guardian 653 in Car Seats section.

Fisher-Price High Chair

See Fisher-Price information under Country Crib in Cribs section.

Books for Parents

All these titles are widely available or can be ordered directly from your bookseller, usually at no extra charge.

Books for Ages 6 Months to 4 Years

See above.

Preemie Products

See text itself for shopping information.

Miscellany

Bow Back Rocker

This is widely distributed to the baby trade. For a store near you call Chatham County, a division of U.S. Furniture Industries at (203) 874-1661 in Connecticut or call (919) 885-8026 in North Carolina.

Ride Rite

See shopping information in Preemie Products section.

Auto Sun Shade

Widely available or can be ordered directly by calling (800) 544-1132.

Tender Touch Video

Available by mail order from:

Healthy Alternatives, Inc.
P.O. Box 3234
Reston, VA 22090
(703) 648-9292

Baby Monitor

See Gerry shopping information under Guardian 653 in the Car Seat section.

Bath Center

See Fisher-Price information under Country Crib in Cribs section.

Little Potty

See Baby Björn shopping information under Travel Cot in Cribs section.

Fisher-Price Potty

See Fisher-Price shopping information under Country Crib in Cribs section.

Bathe & Change

See Baby Björn shopping information under Travel Cot in Cribs section.

Kindergard Safety Products

Widely available nationwide.

Safeguard 285 Vaporizer

Widely available nationwide.

Adjustable Guard Rail

Available in children's specialty stores and some department stores. For the name of a store near you contact:

G.W. Dmka, Inc.
196 Van Winkle Avenue
Garfield, NJ 07026
(201) 478-3222

Nuline Pressure Gate 202

Available in discount stores, department stores, catalog showrooms and children's specialty shops. For information on a store near you contact:

Nuline Industries
P.O. Box 217-214
Nuline Street
Suring, WI 54174
(414) 842-2141

Splat Mat

Widely available.

Athletic Equipment

Spaulding Skill Builders

Widely available nationwide.

Baseball Equipment

Cooper products are widely distributed in sports stores and sports departments. They also put out a catalog. Call 1-800-828-1140 for a free copy. In New York dial 1-800-462-1133.

Nerf Softball

Available in many stores and some sports retailers.

Hockey Equipment

See Cooper information under Baseball.

Aqua Learn

Available in many children's clothing stores or directly from the manufacturer. Contact:

Aqua Learn
932 Parker
Berkeley, CA 94710
(415) 841-9188

Fishing

Orvis puts out a catalog. Call (802) 362-3166 for a copy.

Skiing

Dynastar is widely distributed through ski shops and sporting goods department. Ditto on Salomon.

Tennis

Prince rackets are widely distributed across the country.

Index

D

E

Shannon Gilligan

Shannon Gilligan is the author of twelve children's books, including three bestsellers. Her title *The Case of the Silk King* in the popular Choose-Your-Own-Adventure Series is currently under production for NBC telelvision. Gilligan graduated from Williams College in 1981. She is the founder of Whitbread Books. When she is not traveling to do research for her books, she lives with her family in northern Vermont.

Susan Landsman

Susan Landsman has a master's degree in early childhood and special education from Wheelock College in Boston. After ten years of teaching, she is now editor of the *Parent Press*, a Burlington, Vermont–based publication for families. Her free-lance writing on parenting issues has appeared in newspapers and magazines across the United States.

Susan is the mother of a delightful 3-year-old boy and plans to have another child.